REALIZING
THE
PROMISES
GOD
OF

Beyond Foundational Truths to a Spirit-Filled, In-This-World Faith of Disciplined Obedience to One's Calling

T. C. PINKERTON

WESTBOW
PRESS®
A DIVISION OF THOMAS NELSON
& ZONDERVAN

WestBow Press books may be ordered through booksellers or by contacting:

WestBow Press
A Division of Thomas Nelson & Zondervan
1663 Liberty Drive
Bloomington, IN 47403
www.westbowpress.com
1 (866) 928-1240

ISBN: 978-1-5127-0680-2 (sc)

Library of Congress Control Number: 2015912765

Print information available on the last page.

WestBow Press rev. date: 09/21/2015

To Marilyn
whose loving patience never ends.

"I've come to know and understand more and more the profound this-worldliness of Christianity." … *"By this-worldliness I mean living unreservedly in life's duties, problems, success and failures, experiences and perplexities."* … *"It is only by living completely in this world that one learns to have faith."*

Dietrich Bonhoeffer writing from Tegel Prison, 21 July 1944

CONTENTS

List of Tables

PREFACE

This study of Hebrews Chapter 6 was inspired by Pastor Andrew Paton, senior minister of the Clinton Church of the Nazarene in Clinton, New Jersey. The inspiration came from a sermon on Hebrews 6:13-20 entitled "The Certainty of God's Promises" by Pastor Andrew, preached on August 12, 2012 and sent to me by e-mail. This sermon is highlighted in Lesson 4.

Pastor Andrew is an expository preacher, who originates from South Africa. With this preaching method, he selects a book of the Bible and preaches on that book, passage by passage, from beginning to end without omission. This form of Bible-based, "full-gospel" teaching is a lost art. After each sermon members of the congregation collect in the basement of the church for a "talk-back" session. Pastor Andrew writes a question regarding the sermon on a white board, then he steps back and listens to the feedback. As the discussion progresses, he writes down selected points on the white board and asks additional questions. He verbally connects the feedback, sometimes diagramming the ideas on the board, as people speak. From this exercise a deeper meaning of Scripture is revealed. Months will go by during the expository preaching of the Bible book, so the sessions are inherently connected week to week. It is rare to find a minister with the experience and skill at dynamic conversation to facilitate such a discussion. For a short period of time, while a member of this church, I took notes during these "talk-back" sessions. I would tie together the thoughts expressed and write up a summary, which I would periodically read to the group.

The idea of making a chronicle of this study came from the process described above. A Bible Study Life Group consisting of eleven knowledgeable Christians, meeting in homes twice a month, studied Hebrews Chapter 6, passage by passage, over a period of seven months. My wife and I took notes during the meetings, and afterwards I would write-up the presentation and discussion, attempting to weave together the verbal feedback. Our primary reference was *The Holiest of All* by Andrew Murray, so we divided the passages in Hebrews Chapter 6 among the lessons roughly in accordance with Murray's Chapters: 45, 46, 47, 48 & 49. Having read one of Murray's Chapters, I would prepare a few handouts prior to the meeting. After singing a few hymns and having a short prayer, the meeting would begin by reading selected parts from Murray's book; then we would allow the Holy Spirit to guide us through the discussion, for in Matthew 18:20 Jesus said: "For where two or three are gathered in my name, there am I in the midst of them." After the lesson the group would have a time of intercessory prayer. As we proceeded from month to month, the presentations, discussions, and reflections expanded; as such, the last original lesson was divided into two lessons: one regarding the theology uncovered and one an exercise. The following are the lessons as they evolved from October 2012 to April 2013, where this exegesis unfolded before us. The words in brackets are inserted for clarity.

ACKNOWLEDGMENT

Considerable thanks is extended to each Life Group member who dedicated themselves to participating in the meetings, and who provided feedback during the discussions with relevant scriptures, insights, and interpretations. This includes Alex and Beverly Tchalemian, Bob and Marjorie Folkestad, Mark and Holly Scott, Nick and Ellen Diemel, Kimberley Way, and Marilyn Pinkerton. In addition, my wife Marilyn is thanked for her diligence in taking notes, for her patience in helping to reconstruct the discussions, and for her careful scrutiny with proofing.

Much appreciation is owed Alex Tchalemian for his spiritual wisdom throughout the study. He is credited with explaining the difference between the terms "iniquity" and "transgression" and with discernment of the "unpardonable" sin.

A very special thanks is given to Pastor Andrew Paton who inspired the study, who recommended using Andrew Murray's book *The Holiest of All*, and who took time from his busy schedule to review the manuscript and to offer helpful suggestions.

BIBLE STUDY LIFE GROUP

Members of the Bible Study Life Group attend The Bend Church of the Nazarene in Bend, Oregon. They make up an ecumenical collection of North Americans with diverse origins from varied Christian traditions. Some are U.S. citizens by birth; others are naturalized citizens; while a few are nationals. Origins outside the U.S. include Canada, France (Armenian), The Netherlands, and Indonesia (Dutch). Prior Christian backgrounds include: American Baptist, Disciples of Christ, Free Methodist, United Methodist, Holiness Methodist, Moravian, Evangelical Christian, Lutheran, Armenian Presbyterian, United Presbyterian and Roman Catholic. During this study, every effort was made to interpret the Word of God with the Holy Spirit as our guide, in order to seek out the truth of the Gospel message without being limited by doctrine. It is firmly believed that the theology uncovered may be universally applied by any genuine follower of Christ.

TRANSLATION OF GREEK NEW TESTAMENT

The 1972 edition of *The New Testament in Modern English* by J. B. Phillips is used throughout this study. Compared to previous editions, Phillips said this was "a new translation from the latest and best Greek text published by the United Bible Societies in 1966 and recognized by scholars of all denominations as the best source available". Phillips began translating the New Testament from Greek into modern English in 1941; the first complete translation was made available in 1958. In early versions Phillips put in phrases that may not have been represented by Greek text. By the 1970s he had become "an authority". He said, "I felt I must curb my youthful enthusiasm and *keep as close as I possibly could to the Greek text*". In this last and final edition, regarding the "many extra words which do not occur in the Greek text at all", Phillips said, "I deleted nearly all of them!". His reason for these deletions was "for making the translation not merely readable but as accurate as I could make it". The 1972 edition was intended for use with commentaries, so as Phillips said: "I felt it essential that the scholars who would contribute to such work should have before them the best translation of which I am capable." This particular translation of the Greek New Testament was used during this study, because it is believed to be one of the most accurate translations of the New Testament into English ever produced. Scripture in the text not otherwise marked is from this translation.

INTRODUCTION & OVERVIEW OF HEBREWS

First Life Group Meeting in October 2012
Primary Scripture: Hebrews 6:1-3

Introduction

This is a study of Hebrews Chapter 6, and related scriptures, with the purpose of attempting to answer the following questions:

How does one get beyond the fundamentals of the Christian Faith to accept completely – without reservation – the "spiritual message" of Jesus Christ; whereby, one never stops striving to be more mature in Faith by identifying gifts of the Holy Spirit, discovering the will of God, and realizing God's promises?

How does one become "spiritually adult"?; as noted in Philippians Chapter 3 where Paul said:

Philippians 3:12-16

> Not that I claim to have achieved all this, nor to have reached perfection already. But I keep going on, trying to grasp that purpose of which Christ Jesus grasped me. My brothers, I do not consider myself to have grasped it fully even now. But I do concentrate on this: I forget all that lies behind me and with hands outstretched to whatever lies ahead I go straight for the goal – my reward the honor of my high calling by God in Christ Jesus. All of us who are spiritually adult should think like this, and if at present you think otherwise, yet you will find that God will make even this clear to you. It is important that we go forward in the light of such truth as we have already learned. [1]

T. C. PINKERTON

Overview of Hebrews

<u>Author</u>: The writer of Hebrews was certainly not Paul. The author was a well educated Jewish Christian, who was Greek by birth and who could compose in sophisticated, classical Greek with an extensive Greek vocabulary, unlike Paul. The author apparently had an association with Italian expatriates, who were Christians and who also knew Timothy.

<u>Location writing from</u>: The place of the author is unknown, but it is suspected to have been somewhere in Asia Minor in the Greek speaking world in the same area near Ephesus, where Timothy had been preaching. He was likely among a group of expatriate Italian Jewish Christians on a mission to Asia Minor.

<u>Destination and recipients of letter</u>: The author is writing back to the Jewish Christians of his origin in a large city in Italy, giving greetings to friends and family from these expatriate Italian Jewish Christians, who are with him on a mission away from their homeland.

<u>Timing of letter</u>: The letter is believed to have been written during the latter part of the reign of Nero from 58 to 68 AD, probably around 67 AD. This was a time when Christians back in Italy were coming under persecution.

<u>Reason for writing the letter</u>: The author encourages these Jewish Christians, back home in Italy, to stand firm in the Christian Faith; to let go of the Jewish traditions and associations of the past; to get beyond the fundamentals of the Christian Faith; to understand the deepest meaning of Jesus' spiritual message; to fully accept the Holy Spirit; to clearly understand the meaning of Faith; and to grow into "spiritually adult" Christians.

<u>Themes of the Letter</u>:

- Christ's fulfillment of Old Testament prophecies.
- Christ is superior to angels, prophets, Abraham, Moses, high priests, and to all old traditions (e.g., blood sacrifices, etc.) and all that is in the past.
- To become "spiritually adult" in Christ, one must let go of past things that render a human sense of community security, (i.e., traditions, rituals, associations, etc.) anchoring one in the past, thus preventing growth in Christ.
- Christ is alive in the Holy Spirit. He is a living guide. He is not restricted by things of the past. A "spiritually adult" Christian can rely on the Holy Spirit. Christ is now the eternal High Priest.
- The Jewish Law failed to help even those of exemplary Jewish faith realize the promises – or the ultimate Promise – of God (see Hebrews 11:13 and 11:39).

- The *only* way to become "spiritually adult" and to fully realize the promises of God is living by Faith in Jesus Christ with the Holy Spirit.
- With Christ as our example, endure the suffering of circumstances to which God has called us with genuine patience and Holiness.
- Get beyond the fundamental foundational truths and move on to living by the spiritual guidance of the Holy Spirit.

Getting Beyond the Fundamentals

The writer in Hebrews 6:1-3 challenges his readers to not give up the fundamentals of the Faith, but, while holding onto these foundational truths, to get beyond them and move on to growth in the Holy Spirit. The inference is clear: if Christians are stuck on the fundamentals and depend only on the community of believers for growth, they have reached a plateau and can go no further in spiritual development. They must let go of the past – but not these fundamentals – and depend on themselves alone with Christ – not other people – to act on genuinely motivated Faith and to move forward by allowing the Holy Spirit to dwell within.

Hebrews 6:1-3

> Let us leave behind the elementary teaching about Christ and go forward to adult understanding. Let us not lay over and over again the foundational truths:
>
> - repentance from the deeds which led to [spiritual] death,
> - believing in God,
> - the teaching of baptism and laying-on of hands,
> - belief in the resurrection of the dead,
> - and the final judgment.
>
> No, if God allows, let us go on. [2]

Group Discussion

To understand the "spiritual message" from Christ, spoken of by the writer of Hebrews, we must go back to Genesis and understand how God created us. He created humans in His image, so that they, when fully formed in His image, would consist of a body, a soul, and a spirit.

Alex explained that it is important for us to understand how the Old Testament differentiates between our "iniquity" and our "sin". We are all born out of "iniquity", which is the inherent separation of humans from God as a result of Adam's sin. There is nothing anyone can do by individual or corporate human efforts to reestablish the broken relationship between mankind and God. All of the Jewish Law, all of its sacrifices, all of its nation building, and all of its belief could not reestablish this inherent broken relationship with God and remove the "iniquity".

With His atoning sacrificial death on the cross, as the Messiah prophesied in Scripture, only Christ could remove the "iniquity" and enable God's relationship with mankind to be reestablished. Until Jesus' death and resurrection the Jewish people, down through time, could seek God's forgiveness for their "sins" through various means, (i.e., blood sacrifices, following the Law, honoring the High Priests, etc.), but all of this did not remove the "iniquity". In addition, all the efforts of the Jewish people, however sincere, – either as a group or as individuals – could not bring about a Spirit life within. The potential to "live in the Spirit", that was lost by Adam's disobedience, could not be enabled without Christ's resurrection. This allowed the Holy Spirit to dwell within each Christian, as it did for the first time at Pentecost. Prior to that moment, the only person on earth with the Holy Spirit "living within" was Jesus. His return to heaven enabled the Holy Spirit to come to earth, as "the comforter" residing within each believer.

By accepting Christ's death and resurrection, each individual is reunited with God by the removal of the "iniquity" that separated mankind from God, and each individual is forgiven of the "sins" he has committed. Throughout a Christian's life one can be forgiven of individual sins, if one is genuine in remorse and genuine in repentance. One's "iniquity" can be removed only once. A return to the state of "iniquity" is a permanent separation from God. (Lesson 2)

The Jewish Christians, to which the epistle of Hebrews was addressed, had accepted Christ as the Messiah, who removed the "iniquity" and reunited them with God, but they did not fully understand the "spiritual message" of Christ. They had not been "awakened to the Holy Spirit", so to speak; whereupon, they would have been living by the guidance of the Holy Spirit. Instead, they were continuing to live by the cultural traditions of Judaism, with the knowledge of Christ applied by their human intellectual efforts. In effect, they had been baptized, but they had not experienced within themselves the power of the Holy Spirit. The Word of the New Covenant was not alive in them. They were treating it just as if it was only an extension of the existing Jewish Law, and not as an entirely new way of living. They needed to examine their motives.

Hebrews 4:12

> For the Word that God speaks is alive and active, it cuts more keenly than any two-edged sword: it strikes through to the place where soul and spirit meet, to the innermost intimacies of a man's being: it examines the very thoughts

and motives of a man's heart. No creature has any cover from the sight of God; everything lies naked and exposed before the eyes of Him with whom we have to deal. [3]

To receive the "spiritual message" one must examine the innermost motives that drive one's actions. These Jewish Christians found security in the community and traditions of the Jewish Law. They continued to cling to this lifestyle. This prevented them from growing into spiritual adulthood.

The author of Hebrews makes extensive argument that Christ is superior to all that came before. In order to grow in Christ, it was necessary for these Christians to let go of past religious and social customs, regardless of their previous purpose.

Equally, today we must give up those things of the past which prevent us from growing in Christ. These things may be of a material, social, or psychological nature. We need to look to Scripture to see what Christ calls upon us to give up in order that we might grow.

Satan will continue to work on our minds to make us think that these things, which we hold onto, are materially necessary or psychologically true. With Christ such physical things might not be needed for our security. With Christ such thoughts about ourselves might not be true at all. We must grow to listen to God's discerning voice; so we will know what is of God, what is of ourselves, and what is of Satan.

As for Satan, the only tool he has to attack us is through our minds, so we must know for certain where our thoughts come from and use the resources of the Holy Spirit to defeat them.

II Corinthians 10:3-5

> For though we walk in the flesh, we do not war according to the flesh, for the weapons of our warfare are not of the flesh, but divinely powerful for the destruction of fortresses. We are destroying speculations and every lofty thing raised up against the knowledge of God, and we are taking every thought captive to the obedience of Christ. (NASB)

Psalms 91:1

> He who dwells in the shelter of the Most High will abide in the shadow of the Almighty. (NASB)

Our thoughts are either from God, the Flesh, or the Devil.

1. If the thoughts are from God, they glorify God and they are "Kingdom Style": Love, Humility, Peace, etc., as described in Philippians 4.8.

2. If the thoughts are from the Flesh, they are from "I" and can be wrong thinking about ourselves. These thoughts must be brought before God.

3. If the thoughts are from the Devil, they tend to

   - accuse us
   - deceive us
   - tempt us
   - appeal to our ego or pride
   - attempt to satisfy us
   - condemn us

We must be able to discern where the thoughts come from, so we can deal with them correctly in a manner that honors God. Beyond controlling our thoughts, the writer of Hebrews challenged these Jewish Christians to let go of all things from this world that might be preventing them from growing in Christ (i.e., traditions, culture, rituals, associations, activities, habits, beliefs, etc.).

In addition, the writer was asking that these Jewish Christians stop focusing so much on the fundamentals. These fundamentals were the foundation of their faith and important, but once understood, they needed to move on to living in the Holy Spirit.

Ultimately, the writer had recognized that these Christians were not accepting responsibility for their lives or their own Spiritual growth. They had apparently accepted that just being a part of the local religious community of believers, participating in its community activities, and living a moral life was sufficient to fulfill Christ's message. They did not realize that their individual growth in the Holy Spirit was *their own personal responsibility*, along with their personal relationship with Christ (i.e., no other person could do it for them). They needed to examine the deepest motives of their hearts and come to the understanding that no one but themselves – *as individuals* – with the help of the Holy Spirit, could do those things necessary to grow into full *Spiritual adulthood*.

Each individual is by himself accountable for his own Spiritual growth. He alone must make the decisions and he alone must take the actions that will lead to being "Spiritually adult". Paul said to Timothy:

II Timothy 3:15

> – and that from childhood you have known the sacred writings which are able to give you the wisdom that leads to salvation through faith which is in Christ Jesus. (NASB)

It takes a *personal active effort* on the part of an individual to move forward in growth in the Holy Spirit by fellowship, prayer, remaining in the Word, abiding, listening to God's voice, and *acting on* the Holy Spirit's guidance in those *critical life choices*, that reveal our deepest motives.

The discussion ended with a reading of Philippians 3:12-16 given at the beginning of the lesson.

Conclusion

To become a mature Christian one must "leave behind the elementary teaching *about* Christ and go forward to adult understanding" (Hebrews 6:1) of *experiencing* Christ by allowing oneself to be filled with the Holy Spirit, to trust God fully, and to step out in significant acts of Faith; thereby, encountering the full blessings of God through the fruits of the Holy Spirit.

LESSON 2

THE UNFORGIVABLE SIN

Second Life Group Meeting in October 2012
Primary Scripture: Hebrews 6:4-8

Committing the Unforgivable Sin

The author of Hebrews identified three types of Christians in Chapter 6:

(i) immature Christians, who have not yet realized the power of the Holy Spirit;

(ii) mature Christians, who are filled with and living by the Holy Spirit; and

(iii) "fallen away" Christians who had rejected God, attacked the Holy Spirit, and publicly disgraced the Faith, thus committing the "unforgivable sin".

This sin is both very real and very rare, and it must not be confused with common backsliding.

Hebrews 6:4-8 (underlines below added for text comparison)

> When you find men who have been enlightened, who have tasted the heavenly gift and received the Holy Spirit, who have known the wholesome nourishment of the Word of God and touched the spiritual resources of the eternal world and who then <u>fall away, it proves impossible to make them repent</u> as they did at first. For they are re-crucifying the Son of God in their own souls, and <u>exposing him to contempt</u> (verse 6). Ground which absorbs the rain that often falls on it and produces plants which are useful to those who cultivate it, is ground which has the blessing of God. But ground which produces nothing but thorns and thistles is of no value and is bound sooner or later to be condemned – only thing to do is burn it. ⁴ (Phillips)

> verse 6: and they have <u>fallen away, it is impossible to renew them again to repentance</u>, since they again crucify to themselves the Son of God and <u>put Him to open shame</u>. (NASB)

verse 6: if they <u>fall away, to be brought back to repentance</u>, because to their loss, they are crucifying the Son of God all over again and <u>subjecting him to public disgrace</u>. (NIV)

verse 6: If they then deviate from the faith and <u>turn away from their allegiance, it is impossible to bring them back to repentance</u>, for (because, while, as long as) they nail upon the cross the Son of God afresh as far as they are concerned and are <u>holding Him up to contempt and shame and public disgrace</u>. [5] (AMP)

verse 6: If people who were like that <u>leave their faith in Christ</u>, they <u>cannot come to God again</u>. They themselves nail God's Son up on the cross again. <u>They are holding him up to shame before everyone</u>. [6] (WE)

The author was speaking to the immature Christians in group (i), who had not yet realized the power of the Holy Spirit, about those who had committed the "unforgivable sin". He wanted to make it perfectly clear to these immature Christians that he was *NOT* considering them to be among those in group (iii), who had "fallen away" from Christ by committing the "unforgivable sin" and who "nail upon the cross the Son of God afresh".

This "fallen away" and "re-crucifying the Son of God in their own souls", of which the author speaks in this passage of Hebrews, is extremely serious and cannot be forgiven. It is not simply a backsliding, or losing interest, or becoming sinful again out of human weakness, or having gone back to secular friends, or getting angry with God, or even cursing Christ himself, or engaging in a wrestling match with God, or having committed any sin not involving an attack on the Holy Spirit, etc. These examples of backsliding are "transgressions" which can be forgiven; however, they do not in anyway affect one's salvation or return one to a state of "iniquity". One's "iniquity" has been removed *once and for all* by Christ's atoning death and resurrection. On the other hand, the state of having "fallen away", which is the *only* way one can return to a state of "iniquity", is by committing the so-called unforgivable or "unpardonable" sin.

It is important to understand that in order to commit the "unpardonable" sin one has to have "*known*" the Holy Spirit. One sees in Hebrews 6:4-8 that these men "have been enlightened", "tasted the heavenly gift", "received the Holy Spirit", "*known* ... the Word of God", and "touched the spiritual resources" of heaven. Before committing the "unpardonable" sin, they were in every respect very genuine, saved, sincere, spirit-filled Christians. Equally, one must remember that while Jesus lived on earth he was the only human being to be filled with the Holy Spirit, thus he was the only person to have "*known*" the Holy Spirit. Not until Pentecost did others receive the Holy Spirit, and for the first time its power, comfort, and gifts became "known" to them from within.

There are two times when Jesus revealed the nature of the "unpardonable" sin, which is a *very unique sin against the Holy Spirit*. On these two occasions, some of the Jewish Scribes and Pharisees confronted Jesus after he had performed miraculous healings. Believing His power was from Satan, they decided to condemn the Spirit within Him by openly disgracing the work of Jesus Christ in public and calling His Spirit "unclean".

The first incident is recorded in Mark 3:20-30. At a large gathering of people, some Jewish Scribes claimed that the Spirit within Jesus was of Satan. These Scribes gave credit to Satan for what Jesus was doing in "casting out evil spirits". Jesus elaborates that this is impossible, because a "house divided against itself cannot stand". In verses 28-29, Jesus describes the nature of the "unpardonable" sin.

Mark 3:28-29

> "Truly I say to you, all sins shall be forgiven the sons of men, and whatever blasphemies they utter, but whoever blasphemes against the Holy Spirit never has forgiveness, but is guilty of an eternal sin." (NASB)

Note that Jesus does not specifically direct this at the individual Scribes themselves, but generalizes the proclamation by saying "whoever blasphemes against the Holy Spirit never has forgiveness". This must have perplexed these Scribes greatly, for they must have been saying to one another: Who is this Holy Spirit of whom he speaks? Since these Scribes did not "know" the Holy Spirit, they did not themselves commit the "unpardonable" sin. They did what would have been such a sin, had it been possible for them to have *received* the Holy Spirit and "known" the Holy Spirit from within, which was impossible. Jesus was making a very important point for future reference: saying "all sins", except to "blaspheme against the Holy Spirit", can be forgiven; even blasphemy against Himself or God, but not against the Holy Spirit.

The second time Jesus revealed the unforgivable sin was after he had healed a man who was blind and dumb. This is recorded in Matthew 12:22-32. This time some Jewish Pharisees said the same thing as had the Scribes, that Jesus must have been filled with the power of the devil to perform these miracles. Again, Jesus makes the same pronouncement to the Pharisees, as he did to the Scribes, saying that Satan cannot cast out Satan and any kingdom divided against itself cannot stand. Jesus then repeats the nature of the "unpardonable" sin in Matthew 12:30-32.

Matthew 12:30-32

> "He who is not with Me is against Me; and he who does not gather with Me scatters. Therefore I say to you, any sin and blasphemy shall be forgiven men, but blasphemy against the Spirit shall not be forgiven. And whoever shall

speak a word against the Son of Man, it shall be forgiven him; but whoever shall speak against the Holy Spirit, it shall not be forgiven him, either in this age, or in the age to come." (NASB)

Again, Jesus did not specifically condemn these particular Pharisees, but He generalized it to "whoever shall speak against the Holy Spirit", which had not yet been revealed to the world. Equally, one must remember that on the cross Jesus said, "Forgive them for they know not what they do". Jesus confirmed that the Scribes and Pharisees who spoke against Him and had Him executed, did not know what they were doing, so they could be forgiven.

Returning now to the Christians in group (iii) of Heb. 6:6, who must have done the same thing as these Scribes and Pharisees, we see that they were *not* forgiven, for they had "received the Holy Spirit" and *knew* of its powers and gifts. When speaking out against the Holy Spirit in public, they must have been very conscious of the fact that they were deliberately – as a matter of their "free will" – blaspheming against the Holy Spirit. Attempting to reunite these former Christians with God would be to bring "contempt", "shame", and "public disgrace" to Christ. To commit the "unpardonable" sin returns one back to the state of "iniquity", thus separating oneself from God permanently.

This is not something that any Christian can do easily, or by accident, or by some inadvertent consequence, or in some moment of weakness, or in a moment of anger, or by some indiscretion. It is something done deliberately, conscientiously, with malice of forethought, with a very hardened heart, after considering the consequences carefully, after stifling and rejecting the Holy Spirit within, after meditating at some length on the action to be taken, and after killing one's own conscience. This is not anything a dedicated Christian would do, for the Holy Spirit would be working overtime to prevent a decision that would lead to an irreversible action. This rare sin likely starts as a habit and leads to a lifestyle. [7]

This action requires that one has the ability to discern the presence of the Holy Spirit within other people – as well as themselves – and to recognize those people bringing about the will of God through the power of the Holy Spirit. To commit the "unforgivable sin" one must become jealous and hateful of these Holy Spirit filled Christians doing the work of God in public. It is almost impossible to think that such a person could have been a genuine Holy Spirit filled Christian; however, this is exactly what the author of Hebrews infers by his passage.

During this time of Nero's reign, one can only assume that the persecution of Christians by the Romans had reached such a level that some Jewish Christians might have thought it safer to reject Christianity entirely and to return to the old Jewish community.

T. C. PINKERTON

By dissociating themselves completely from their former Christian believers, they made it clear to Roman authorities that they were not one of these Christians. Rather, they were on the side of the Romans in working against these Christians, who would not worship emperor Nero as a God. They must have felt the need to demonstrate to the Romans whose side they were on. If a Holy Spirit filled Christian was doing God's work in public and if one of these former ungodly believers seized the opportunity to openly attack the Holy Spirit in these other Christians, then a sin against the Holy Spirit and the "unpardonable" sin was committed. To do this in front of other Romans proved their allegiance and regained a standing in the old Jewish community, which must have been a safe haven. These are the former Christians in group (iii) who have "fallen way".

Group Discussion

A Word to the Immature Christians

The author of Hebrews is telling the Christians in group (i), who are immature, that they must get beyond just "talking" about God and Christ, and begin "walking" with God, as those in group (ii). He tells these Jewish Christians that they are not the ones in group (iii), who have "fallen away" and who are now beyond forgiveness.

Those who Committed the Unforgivable Sin

The Christians in group (iii) who have committed the "unpardonable" sin and who are now completely "fallen away" from Christ have blasphemed the Holy Spirit. They have not merely committed another forgivable "transgression", but they have returned to the state of "iniquity". They had openly, before men, denied Christ and the Holy Spirit.

Remember what Jesus said about denying him before men. To blaspheme the Holy Spirit is to "deny" Christ, who enables the Holy Spirit. Jesus said:

Matthew 10:33

> "But whoever shall deny Me before men, I will also deny him before My Father who is in heaven." (NASB)

The Apostle Paul explained in his letter to the Romans:

Romans 10:9-10

> – that if you confess with your mouth Jesus *as* Lord, and believe in your heart that God raised Him from the dead, you will be saved; for with the heart

man believes, resulting in righteousness, and with the mouth he confesses, resulting in salvation. (NASB)

We should never forget that the Holy Spirit is our "comforter", protector, and connection to God through Jesus Christ.

The Pharisees and Scribes knew the Law, but they were not "born-again". If they turned away, it was of no consequence to them. They had the knowledge of God and Christ, by way of ancient prophesy and by way of observing Jesus (yet not recognized), but not the Holy Spirit. The Pharisee's and Scribe's speech and actions had "crossed the line", but they themselves had not.

Some Jews went back to the Jewish community to be safe from the Romans and were no longer Christians. They gave their full allegiance to Rome and worshiped Roman gods. They had "fallen away" and committed the "unpardonable" sin.

In Matthew 16:16 when Peter declared of Jesus: "Thou art the Christ, the Son of the living God"; the Holy Spirit was "on him" but not "in him". That is why, a few moments later, in Matthew 16:23, after Peter said he would not allow Jesus to be physically harmed, as He had just described; Jesus said, "Get thee behind me Satan". Prior to Christ's crucifixion the Holy Spirit could be "on" Peter – or anyone else – while the spirit of Satan was still "in him".

Equally, when Peter is said to have disowned Christ three times, after he was taken prisoner, he did not commit the "unpardonable" sin, because he did not yet "know" the Holy Spirit. As such, he did not blaspheme the Holy Spirit. Satan and the Holy Spirit cannot exist in a person at the same time.

In a moment of weakness or anger or frustration or immaturity, a Christian can say things "against" God or Christ, but without necessarily "denying" Him altogether. Such Christians can be redeemed by the Holy Spirit. Marjorie put it plainly, when she said, "If you are worried about committing the 'unpardonable' sin, then you haven't."

By contrast, those former Christians in group (iii), who had openly blasphemed the Holy Spirit in public, had joined Satan in the battle against Christ. They had completely changed sides in the universal spiritual struggle. They could not be forgiven, for they would not "acknowledge God any longer". God gave them back over to a "depraved mind", as Paul observed in Romans1:28-29.

Romans 1:28-29

> And just as they did not see fit to acknowledge God any longer, God gave them over to a depraved mind, to do those things which are not proper, being

> filled with all unrighteousness, wickedness, greed, evil; full of envy, murder, strife, deceit, malice; they are gossips – (NASB)

It takes some time and thought before a former "backsliding" Christian might completely revert back to the state of "iniquity" by openly "denying" and having completely "fallen away" from Christ with a speaking out – or through an action that speaks – in a public attack against the Holy Spirit by way of a very conscious decision to turn against Christ.

Paul was referring to this decision-making process in his letter to the Galatians, when he learned of Christians thinking about completely "falling away". He recognized that some Galatians were considering going back to honoring humans above Christ, through their actions, which would acknowledge the old Jewish practices and rituals as being superior to Christ. Paul said to them, "Did you doubt your first experience with the Holy Spirit?" He hoped to bring them back into a state of grace by honoring the Holy Spirit before they did something foolish, such as blaspheming against the Holy Spirit in public, which could not be reversed.

Paul said:

Galatians 1:6-10

> I am astonished that you are so quickly deserting the one who called you by the grace of Christ and are turning to a different gospel — which is really no gospel at all. Evidently some people are throwing you into confusion and are trying to pervert the gospel of Christ. But even if we or an angel from heaven should preach a gospel other than the one we preached to you, let him be eternally condemned! As we have already said, so now I say again: If anybody is preaching to you a gospel other than what you accepted, let him be eternally condemned! Am I now trying to win the approval of men, or of God? Or am I trying to please men? If I were still trying to please men, I would not be a servant of Christ. (NIV)

Comments about the Jewish Christians in Hebrews

It appears that the immature Jewish Christians, to whom the author of Hebrews is speaking, may not yet have given full allegiance to the Holy Spirit. They were still potentially vulnerable to circumstances or to arguments that might have drawn them back into the ways of their old human natures. They needed to get beyond the simple immature *talking about* the fundamentals of Faith and move on to a mature *experiencing* of Christ by a complete surrender to the Holy Spirit. The author does not consider that they have foolishly "fallen away" by committing a sin against the Holy Spirit, as have those who are now beyond salvation.

The Life Group expressed that to be a mature Christian one must give up the desires of "human nature", that are driven by self-interest, and substitute Christ's "divine nature", that is driven by the Holy Spirit, as noted in II Peter 1:4-8. The power of the Holy Spirit gives one the ability to exercise self-control over "human nature", if one allows the Holy Spirit to work within to exercise "*the* divine nature".

II Peter 1:4-8

> For by these He has granted to us His precious and magnificent promises, in order that by them you might become partakers of *the* divine nature, having escaped the corruption that is in the world by lust. Now for this very reason also, applying all diligence, in your faith supply moral excellence, and in *your* moral excellence, knowledge, and in *your* knowledge, self-control, and in *your* self-control, perseverance, and in *your* perseverance, godliness; and in *your* godliness, brotherly kindness, and in *your* brotherly kindness, love. For if these *qualities* are yours and are increasing, they render you neither useless nor unfruitful in the true knowledge of our Lord Jesus Christ. (NASB)

There are clear differences between a Christian and a non-Christian: being saved, getting "rid of one's worst enemy – self", asking for forgiveness, etc. The characteristics between different levels of Christians and non-Christians should be explored further. (see expanded list in Lesson 3 and in Appendix I)

It is not "do's and don'ts", but a relationship with Christ that makes one a true Christian. Of course, divine relationships may be strong, maturing, and growing or weak, declining, and short-lived, as in the Parable of the Sower (Matthew 13:1-23).

Alex gave an example of a woman who came to his Bible study with a list of "do's and don'ts", desiring a confirmation of which were acceptable or unacceptable. Alex challenged her with the question: "Do you love your husband?" She said, "Yes". Next he asked, "Would you do anything to hurt him? She said, without hesitation, "No". Alex then explained, "That's what it's like to love Christ." He enumerated that it is as simple as that. We are saved by the Spirit; we begin as babes in the Spirit; we are sanctified in the soul; and we are glorified in death. When we sin, we ask for forgiveness and we are restored. Alex further elaborated: "There is salvation of the spirit, soul, and body. These must be kept separate if we are to grow spiritually. Adam had a sixth sense, his Spirit, before he sinned. After that he only had his five senses."

Of course, one's five physical senses are seeing, hearing, tasting, feeling, and smelling. One's sixth sense, which connects us with God, is not physical but spiritual. Without faith in and a relationship with Jesus Christ the restoration of this sense by way of the Holy Spirit is impossible. The development of this sixth sense with the Holy Spirit, as our resource, is the primary key to maturing as a Christian and becoming "sanctified".

When Jesus said to love the Lord thy God with all thy *heart*, *mind*, *soul*, and *strength*, it is clear that these elements must be separate entities; or He would not have separated them into a series. They are, of course, not independent of one another but interrelated. It may be worth exploring in a later lesson the difference between each of these parts. That is, emotions and motivations are of the *heart*. "Have you had a *heart* change?", one might ask. Thinking, intellect, understanding, and memory are of the *mind*. The Spirit is clearly of the *soul*. "Are you saving '*souls*'?", one might say. One is either filled with the Holy Spirit or without it — empty. The *soul* is the deepest part of our ability to discern truth. "Is one's *soul* 'lost' or 'restored'?", one might inquire. *Strength* cuts across the *heart*, *mind*, and *soul*, because *strength* can be physical, mental, or spiritual. It was noted by the Life Group, that when the Holy Spirit comes into an individual, this Spirit of God brings these human elements into alignment with the will of God, as they were in the beginning of time, before Adam's sin of "iniquity". This means that Christ's atonement is a "done deal" (removing the "iniquity"), but to realize the benefits of the Holy Spirit within ourselves, one must accept the *individual responsibility* of growing and maturing in Faith by cultivating one's relationship with Christ.

Transgressions of the Unforgiving

Regarding "transgressions", however, that could be another story. A member noted the Lord's Prayer is the example of forgiveness when it says, "and forgive us our debts, as we also have forgiven our debtors". Jesus said immediately after giving the Lord's prayer in Matthew 6:14-15 that one *must* forgive others to be forgiven. Personal lack of forgiveness is a sign of insincere repentance. [8]

Matthew 6:14-15

> "For if you forgive men for their transgressions, your heavenly Father will also
> forgive you. But if you do not forgive men, then your Father will not forgive
> your transgressions." (NASB)

The group discussed briefly what it might mean to get to heaven without some "transgressions" being forgiven. Such "transgressions" do not negate one's salvation, but they must have some impact on one's eternal life. No one had a good answer. This remains a mystery, for Scripture does not speak much about degrees of "rewards in heaven" or about *how* the "heavenly mansions" are being prepared. No one seemed to know what it might mean, if one arrives in heaven "smoking", as it was so well put by a group member.

Alex said if you can't forgive someone who has harmed you, then God can't forgive you. That is, you *won't* be forgiven for that particular transgression; so this will limit the

Holy Spirit. The Holy Spirit wants to fill us and impart to us the "gifts of the Spirit", but if we have unforgiving hearts, we are blocked from being completely filled. As such, we cannot come to full Spiritual maturity, be fully sanctified, and fully enjoy the fruits of the Spirit, either in this age or the one to come.

More than One Way to Blaspheme the Holy Spirit?

Returning to the topic of the "unpardonable" sin, Holly challenged the group to consider whether there was more that one way to blaspheme the Holy Spirit and to commit the "unforgiveable sin". Although the group did not have time to discuss this, it is worth considering.

Blaspheming the Holy Spirit is speaking out against Him in public as He is at work doing the will of God.

It is often said that "actions can speak louder than words". In the case of the Galatians, the issue was a ritual; if they performed, "Christ would no longer be of any use to them." If they performed the old Jewish rituals to be a part of the old Jewish community by honoring the Law, they would be putting the Law above Christ, thus "denying" His authority and His gift of the Holy Spirit. In doing so, they were making a conscious decision to act before the public as "denying" Christ. Is this blasphemy against the Holy Spirit, as one is speaking by his actions to the public to be against what Christ offers?

Equally, one might consider some who call themselves "evangelists", but who cast off the beliefs of their previous Spirit-filled salvation. They embrace other religions and become theosophists; whereby, manufacturing little more than philosophies of life with Jesus as only one wise person, who can impart some truth but not all moral truth. They claim that Jesus has no divine power; that he is not the "Son of God"; that he cannot impart a Holy Spirit; that the Bible is not the "Word of God" but only a collection of human "narratives"; that Jesus does not perform miracles; and that Jesus is just a very wise Jewish "sage". They write books, they preach sermons, they teach at universities a message that is clearly against the Holy Spirit. One can ask: Are these not blasphemies against the Holy Spirit?

One might say that "God only knows", if these examples, or others, that speak by actions are sins against the Holy Spirit. Of course, no one knows for sure. However, Jesus made it quite clear that *speaking out against the Holy Spirit in public by church leaders through open verbalization is an "unpardonable" sin.* One can imagine, that blasphemy against the Holy Spirit by deeds that "speak" (i.e., books, symbolic acts, boastful behavior, etc.), might equally be "unpardonable" sins.

THE PROMISE SEEKING BELIEVER

**Life Group Meetings in November 2012
Primary Scripture: Hebrews 6:9-12**

Becoming a Mature Christian

The author of Hebrews directs the "immature" Jewish Christians in group (i), to whom he is writing, not to be concerned about those in group (iii), who have "fallen away" and committed the unforgivable sin; but to turn their attention towards their own spiritual growth and maturity in the Faith to join those in group (ii).

Reiterating the conclusion of Lesson 1, the author of Hebrews encourages these Jewish Christians to become "mature" Christians. He tells them that to do this they must "leave behind the elementary teaching *about* Christ and go forward to adult understanding" (Hebrews 6:1). They must not continue to "lay over and over again the foundational truths", but to "go on" to *build* on these foundational truths. This is done by taking on Christ's commandments in obedient Faith and *applying* them to real-life, everyday circumstances where one must trust God, live a moral life, and step out in Faith. The author is trying to get these immature Christians to stop just talking *about* Christ "over and over again", or just serving him by a commitment to worship, or just practicing the "fundamentals"; but to get out and *experience* Christ in one's own personal life. As expressed so clearly by Alex, during the Life Group discussion, the key difference between individuals in these two groups (i) & (ii) is whether one is dedicated to doing God's will by an expression of only "brotherly love" through human efforts, as those in group (i), or whether one shares in Christ's suffering by fulfilling God's will by practicing self-sacrificing "*agape* love" through the power of the Holy Spirit, as those in group (ii).

To *experience* Christ and *share* in His suffering one must

(i) be filled with the Holy Spirit,
(ii) trust God fully,

(iii) surrender one's self-will to God's will,

(iv) genuinely live a moral life with utmost honesty,

(v) care about others more than self,

(vi) abide through prayer and forgiveness, and

(vii) step out in personal acts of Faith that might lead to "longsuffering".

Individual voluntarily acts of Faith on the part of these "mature" Christians of group (ii) enable relationship building with Christ that brings on the full blessings of God through the fruits of the Holy Spirit. This is not reached, however, without strengthening the soul by way of discipline, diligence, and perseverance during periods of "longsuffering". [9] The "full possession of the promise" and the bringing on of "better things" with its joy of the "full experience of salvation" and a "full assurance of hope" in the full blessings of heavenly rewards that can accompany eternal life, requires a refining and an annealing (i.e., making stronger) by fire with a "perseverance of faith" through "longsuffering" that "strengthens the soul". [10] This is seen in Hebrews 6:9-12 in three translations below:

Hebrews 6:9-12 (underline added for text comparison)

> But although we give these words of warning we feel sure that you, whom we love, are capable of <u>better things</u> and will enjoy the <u>full experience of salvation</u>. God is not unfair: he will not lose sight of all that you have done, nor of the <u>loving labor</u> which you have shown for his sake in <u>looking after fellow-Christians</u> (as you are still doing). It is our earnest wish that every one of you should show a similar keenness in fully <u>grasping the hope</u> that is <u>within you</u>, until the end. We do not want any of you to grow slack, but to follow the example of those who through sheer patient faith came to possess the promises. [11] (Phillips)

> But beloved, we are convinced of <u>better things</u> concerning you, and things that <u>accompany salvation</u>, though we are speaking in this way. For God is not unjust so as to forget your <u>work and the love</u> which you have shown <u>toward His name</u>, in having ministered and in still <u>ministering to the saints</u>. And we desire that each one of you show the same <u>diligence</u> so as to realize the <u>full assurance of hope</u> until the end, that you may not be sluggish, but imitators of those who through faith and patience inherit the promises. (NASB)

> But, beloved, we are persuaded <u>better things</u> for you, and things that <u>accompany salvation</u>, though we thus speak: for God is not unrighteous to forget <u>your work and the love</u> which ye shewed [sic] toward his name, in that ye <u>ministered unto the saints</u>, and still do minister. And we desire that each one of you may shew [sic] the same <u>diligence</u> unto the <u>fullness of hope</u> even to the end; that ye be not sluggish, but imitators of them who through faith and patience (longsuffering) inherit the promises. [12] (RV)

T. C. PINKERTON

In his treatise on Hebrews, *The Holiest of All*, Andrew Murray places emphasis on the word *diligence* as he contrasts those "immature" Christians of group (i), who "pass into a life of ease", versus the "mature" ones of group (ii), who embrace "self-sacrifice". Murray says:

> In all worldly business, diligence is the secret to success. Without attention and trouble and hearty effort, we cannot expect our work to prosper. And yet, there are many Christians who imagine that in the Christian life things will come right of themselves. When they are told that Jesus undertakes to do all, they count this as a pass into a life of ease. **Truly, no**. His own spirit of self-sacrifice and devotion to the Father's will; His own readiness to forsake all ease and comfort to please God and man; His own unwearying [sic] diligence in working while it was day. And so, our writer urges his readers to show the same diligence they had formerly manifested, *"unto the fullness of hope even to the end."* (Hebrews 3:6) [13]

Murray goes on to explain how hope lives in the promises gained by perseverance of Faith, as he sees the combination of diligence and hope in Hebrews 3:14, 4:11, and 6:11. He exclaims:

> The great marks of Christian perseverance are here once again joined together. Hope looks again forward and lives in the promises; it glories beforehand in the certainty of their fulfillment. Bright hopefulness is one of the elements of a healthy Christian life – one of the surest preservatives against backsliding. This hopefulness must be cultivated; diligence must be given unto the fullness of hope – a hope that embraces all the fullness of God's promises and that fills all the heart. And all this to the end, with a patience and perseverance that knows no weariness, that waits on God's time and seeks in patience until the fulfillment has come. [14]

Murray further emphasizes the importance of "longsuffering" when he says:

> Longsuffering is the perseverance of faith. Faith grasps at once all that God promises but is in danger of relaxing its hold. Longsuffering comes to tell how faith needs daily to be renewed; it strengthens the soul, even when the promise tarries, still to hold fast, firm unto the end. This is one of the great practical lessons of our epistle and one that the young believer especially needs. Conversion is but a beginning, a step, an entrance on the path. Day by day, its surrender must be renewed; every day, faith must afresh accept Christ and find its strength in Him. Through faith and longsuffering, we inherit – enter into the possession of – the promises. [15]

Murray believes there are "two classes" of Christians: Those who are "content with deliverance" (the majority) and those "who give themselves up with their whole hearts to seek and serve God" (the minority). The writer of Hebrews says the former are the "immature" ones of group (i) and the latter are the "mature" ones of group (ii). Both groups know salvation and practice the "fundamentals" of the Faith, but only the latter group is "striving for the full possession of the promise". [16] Those in group (i) are satisfied with the gift of eternal life, while those in group (ii) are on a quest for "better things", beyond this eternal gift of Christ's work, towards seeking the heavenly rewards promised to those, who by self-sacrifice, diligence, and perseverance show a "labor of love" (i.e., *agape* love), which God will not forget. One can contrast some characteristics of these two groups, as shown in Table I below. They may be referred to as Salvation Satisfied believers versus Promise Seeking believers.

Table I – Contrast between Salvation Satisfied vs. Promise Seeking Believers

Salvation Satisfied believer (majority)	Promise Seeking believer (minority)
saved, acknowledges sin, repents, asks for forgiveness, engages in church activities, but is a *less* mature Christian as follows:	saved, acknowledges sin, repents, asks for forgiveness, engages in church activities, but is a *more* mature Christian as follows:
has not fully surrendered self	strives daily to surrender self
satisfied with "fundamentals" of the Faith	seeks to go beyond "fundamentals"
holds to security of myths & rituals	given over to Holy Spirit within
obeys Christ's 1st & 2nd commandment	obeys Christ's 1st, 2nd & 3rd commandment
does God's will by showing brotherly love	does God's will by brotherly & *agape* love
moral standards aligned with others	personally sets moral standards very high
cannot discern "message" from Holy Spirit	can hear God "speak" through Holy Spirit
weak prayer life	strong prayer life
some "fruits" of the Spirit	many "fruits" of the Spirit
ignorant of his Spiritual Gifts	knows and uses his Spiritual Gifts
may not believe in miracles or has seen few	has experienced miracles — first hand
Faith worked out mostly in church service	Faith worked out mostly in personal life
dedicated to service but takes few risks	goes beyond service to personal risks
has limits to degree of self-sacrifice	prepared for any self-sacrifice
primarily focused on earthly outcomes	focused on heavenly rewards & eternal life
walks with Christ and reaches plateau	strives for "perfection" in Christ
honors God as it builds one's reputation	wholeheartedly seeks to honor God in all
life decisions minimize own suffering	life decisions may lead to "longsuffering"
receives the gift of eternal life	enters heaven with Promise's full reward

Note: Not to be over simplified by these two groupings, one might differentiate among other groups by similar categorical characteristics, as shown in Appendix I.

Group Discussion

The Life Group discussion focused on attempting to get a better understanding of what it meant to experience "longsuffering". Some expressed how difficult it was to persevere in times of hardship and to know that Christ was "with you" during these times. It was noted that one's Faith has nothing to do with one's feelings. A mature Christian should not measure the presence of Christ within (i.e., the Holy Spirit) by any feelings, whatsoever. The group thought it very important during difficult times to stay in the Word and abide in fervent prayer to remain fully connected to the Holy Spirit within. Daily communion with God was seen as a necessity to refresh the Spirit.

"Longsuffering" was seen as a practical means of developing the "discipline" of abiding in Faith through diligence and perseverance of reading the Word, praying, and listening to God for guidance. The group returned to Murray's definition that states: "*Longsuffering is the perseverance of faith.*" Equally, it was reiterated what Murray said that "longsuffering strengthens the soul."

The circumstances that bring on "longsuffering" were noted as transpiring from a believer's voluntary decision to step out in an act of Faith in response to a situation or opportunity presented to him upon "hearing" a message from God, through the Holy Spirit, that God had directed him to personally pursue in accordance with a fulfillment of His will. Whether or not one responds to such a "calling", through a clear voluntary free-choice, is entirely up to the individual, for such steps of Faith incorporate an element of self-sacrifice. These life-critical, faith-decision choices always involve caring for others (e.g., a family member, a close friend, another believer, a person in need, etc.) more than one might care for oneself. The opportunity might take the believer in a direction he might not have been particularly interested in going. In such situations, stepping out in Faith and caring for others by such direct personal self-sacrifice, might bring on "longsuffering" to which Scripture refers. Equally, one might be caught up in circumstances beyond his control. Regardless of the situation, by doing "what is right" – *as perceived by God's will* – events might lead one into "longsuffering".

One must contrast these types of genuine spiritual "longsuffering" against the troubles that one might encounter as a consequence of some sin. If someone suffers, for however long, as a result of a committed sin, even though God's forgiveness is given; consequences that are deserving do not count as the righteous "longsuffering", brought on by voluntary self-sacrifice or circumstances beyond one's control, to which the writer of Hebrews speaks. Such "longsuffering" might be seen as a spiritual gift to the believer as an opportunity to share in Christ's suffering, which, if endured with diligence and perseverance, will surely bring about heavenly rewards.

Marjorie referred the group to Philippians 3:8-12, where the Apostle Paul reflects on his own "longsuffering", brought on by his personal faith-decision to preach to the gentiles. Paul said in the Scripture below:

Philippians 3:8-12

> More than that, I count all things to be loss in view of the surpassing value of knowing Christ Jesus my Lord, for whom I have suffered the loss of all things, and count them but rubbish in order that I may gain Christ, and may be found in Him, not having a righteousness of my own derived from the Law, but that which is through faith in Christ, the righteousness which comes from God on the basis of faith, that I may know Him, and the power of His resurrection and the fellowship of His sufferings, being conformed to His death; in order that I may attain to the resurrection of the dead. Not that I have already obtained it, or have already become perfect, but I press on in order that I may lay hold of that for which also I was laid hold of by Christ Jesus. (NASB)

The group felt that "dying to self", through giving up the "things" of this world, was a key element in a Promise Seeking believer so striving for "perfection in Christ". It was noted that to be "perfect" in Christ was not the perfection of this world, that might be seen as measured by earthly standards, but rather by striving to be more like Christ. John Wesley was a firm believer in a Christian striving for "perfection in Christ". He warns, however, that one must be careful not to get caught up in visible expectations that might reflect with pride on the believer so striving. To "become perfect" in Christ, as Paul so desired, is to humbly seek to do God's will in everything one does and to become wholeheartedly genuine in one's Faith. As such, much seeking might be done in private. Even after all that the Apostle Paul had done, through the power of the Holy Spirit, to have "suffered the loss of all things"; he saw it was necessary to further "press on" in "diligence" and "perseverance" to "lay hold" to the fulfillment of the Promise that "lies ahead".

This diligent type of faith-in-action Promise Seeking believer, guided by the Holy Spirit, is far different from those who consciously choose by their inaction to remain quiescent and satisfied with the "fundamentals" of the Faith. The writer of Hebrews is encouraging his readers to become more like Paul; to listen to the leadings of the Holy Spirit; to step out in real acts of Faith; to endure "longsuffering" with "diligence" and "perseverance"; and to strive to "become perfect" in Christ. In so doing, believers experience Christ through the power of the Holy Spirit and "enter into the possession" of the promises of God.

A very important distinction of a Promise Seeking believer is understanding and practicing the third commandment of Christ. We know the first commandment of Christ is to "love the Lord thy God with all thy heart, mind, soul and strength"; and the second commandment, which was like unto it, is to "love thy neighbor as thyself". Jesus said that the ultimate Spirit of the Law was summed up in these two commandments. However, in spite of that, Jesus gave His third commandment to His disciples at the Last Supper, soon after Judas had departed from the gathering. Jesus said: "A new commandment I give you, that you love one another, even as I have loved you, that you also love one another. By this all men will know that you are My disciples, if you have love for one another." (John 13:34-35, NASB) Jesus went on to say: "If you abide in Me, and My words abide in you, ask whatever you wish, and it shall be done for you. By this is My Father glorified, that you bear much fruit, and so prove to be My disciples." (John 15:7-8, NASB) Jesus further exclaimed this new commandment when He said: "This is My commandment, that you love one another, just as I have loved you. Greater love has no one than this, that one lay down his life for his friends. You are My friends, if you do what I command you. No longer do I call you slaves, for the slave does not know what his master is doing; but I have called you friends, for all things I have heard from My father I have made known to you." (John 15:12-15, NASB)

After Judas left the room, Jesus gave this new commandment *only* to his disciples: those closest to him who he considered his "friends"; because they (i) abided in him, (ii) his words were in them, and (iii) they did what he commanded. This new commandment means that these "friends", who know "all things" that Jesus heard from God, as given in His Word, should love each other as "friends" even to the point of giving up one's life. This new commandment called upon his "friends" to *sacrifice themselves* for each other by showing the same *agape* love that He was about to show by dying on the cross. Ultimately, a Promise Seeking believer is one of Jesus' "friends" if he abides; if he remains in the Word; if he does God's will by faith-action decisions through the leadings of the Holy Spirit; and if he endures to the end by "diligence", "perseverance", "patience", and "longsuffering" brought on by faith-action decisions. Jesus gave these new instructions of voluntary self-sacrifice among mature believers so their blessings would be complete. He pronounced, "These things I have spoken to you, that my joy may be in you, and that your joy may be made full." (John 15:11, NASB)

It was noted that the Promise Seeking believer must be clearly aware that the rewards of self-sacrificing "longsuffering", brought on by faith-action decisions, cannot, for the most part, be realized in this world. One can see in Hebrews Chapter 11, where the author brings to mind the faith of Abel, Enoch, Noah, Abraham, Sarah, Isaac, Jacob, Joseph, Moses, Rahab, Gideon, Barak, Samson, Jephthah, David, Samuel, and the prophets. These great believers in Faith did not receive their rewards on earth, for it is said that "all these died in faith, without receiving the promises, but having seen them and having welcomed them from a distance, and having confessed that they were strangers and exiles on the earth." (Hebrews 11:13) Further the writer of Hebrews tells us: "and all these, having gained approval through their faith, did not receive what was promised, because God had provided something better for us, so that apart from us they should not be made perfect." (Hebrews 11:39-40)

In closing, Ellen referred the group to Galatians 2:20. Here Paul enunciates the ultimate goal of striving to become "perfect in Christ". This goal is realized when one allows Christ within to dominate his being by crucifying self through "longsuffering" as a wholehearted expression of Christ's character. As Paul put it:

Galatians 2:20

> I have been crucified with Christ; and it is no longer I who live, but Christ lives in me; and the *life* which I now live in the flesh I live by faith in the Son of God, who loved me, and delivered Himself up for me. (NASB)

My Anchor Holds [17]
(three verses)

W. C. Martin and Daniel B. Towner
Hymn of the 19th and 20th Century

Tho' the angry surges roll,
On my tempest driven soul,
I am peaceful, for I know,
Wildly though the winds may blow,
I've an anchor safe and sure,
That can evermore endure.

Refrain

And it holds, my anchor holds;
Blow your wildest, then O gale,
On my bark so small and frail.
By His grace I shall not fail.
For my anchor holds, my anchor holds.

I can feel the anchor fast,
As I meet each sudden blast,
And the cable, though unseen,
Bears the heavy strain between.
Thro' the storm I safely ride,
Till the turning of the tide.

Troubles almost 'whelm the soul;
Grief like billows o'er me roll;
Tempters seek to lure astray;
Storms obscure the light of day.
But in Christ I can be bold;
I've an anchor that shall hold.

BUILDING OUR LIFE-LINE TO CHRIST

Life Group Meetings in December 2012 and January 2013
Primary Scripture: Hebrews 6:13-15

Primary Sources

1. The lesson uses Chapter 47 on Hebrews 6:13-15, entitled "Inheriting the Promise", form *The Holiest of All* by Andrew Murray.
2. "The Certainty of God's Promises" by Pastor Andrew Paton of the Clinton Church of the Nazarene, Clinton, NJ, is a sermon delivered on August 12, 2012. The lesson refers to Part A of this sermon on Heb 6:13-15.

Anchoring the Soul

After reading pastor Andrew Paton's sermon, which he sent to me by e-mail in the summer of 2012, I was inspired that he had captured the writer of Hebrews essence of what a Promise Seeking Christian must do to inherit the promises of God. I was excited that this part of Hebrews gives one the actual means God designed for believers to "go beyond the fundamentals" of salvation to seek out the full promises of God, available here on Earth in part and in eternity in full.

Salvation is a gift, and many, as they so choose, may rest on that salvation. Others, however, may wish to seek a deeper walk with Christ by going beyond the gift of salvation and to strive to "become perfect" in Christ, as Paul said. If one so wishes to embark on such a journey, the question remains: Well, how do I do that? Here the writer of Hebrews makes a clear distinction between what one may call Salvation Satisfied Christians and Promise Seeking Christians. As well, he provides the mechanism or method by which one may become more "mature" as he "becomes perfect" in Christ. After reading pastor Andrew's sermon, the Holy Spirit inspired me to write in the margin of the first page seven progressive steps: (i) learn to listen to God, (ii) learn to trust in God, (iii) learn to take real faith-action steps, (iv) learn to wait patiently, (v)

T. C. PINKERTON

learn to hold on to the verbalized promises, (vi) never give up hope, and (vii) take joy in your persecutions, for your reward in heaven is great.

In preparing this lesson, I felt a need to simplify, or reduce to an alternative list of action verbs, the steps that encompass most of the things that Christ has called upon us to DO as a "mature" Christian, if one chooses a closer walk with Him. It is worth reiterating, that such a closeness with Christ is purely voluntary. It is one's own free-choice to engage in such a journey, and it is entirely up to the individual how far he wishes to go. Equally, if anyone so chooses not to seek a closer walk with Jesus, they may remain satisfied with Christ's gift of salvation and eternal life, without a complete fulfillment of the Promise. Jesus made it clear that in heaven the first will be last and the last will be first; that He has gone to prepare a place for each of us; and that there are many mansions in heaven. We should not forget what he said to the woman who asked that her sons be at Jesus' side in heaven. Jesus said, "You do not know what you are asking". In effect, to be by His side means a person must undergo on earth the very same suffering as Jesus Himself.

These statements make it emphatically clear, whether one chooses to believe them or not, that positions in heaven relative to Christ and the degree of "inheritance" of the Promise will differ. In a will the owner of property may dispense his wealth to his descendants in accordance with his pleasing and to his servants according to their "good and faithful" service. The Bible makes it plain that Christ has the authority to do the same. It is equally appropriate to remember that a person cannot select descendants, but they can select their servants. The gift of salvation is available to anyone who chooses to believe in Christ, but those who Christ selects from among believers to accomplish His special duties on earth may be those who have sought to go beyond the fundamentals and to seek a closer walk with Him. These are the Promise Seeking believers.

After writing down the first five steps (shown below), I underlined the first letter of each action verb; then I looked for an acronym. In a dictionary I found – to my surprise – it created the word hawse, which I had never heard. To hawse is to bring up the anchor of a ship. Hawse comes from an Anglo-French sailing term *hauceur,* which was derived from the French word *hausser,* meaning to raise or hoist. A hawser (hô'zer) is a large rope in the bow of a ship to which an anchor is attached.

What came to mind was the old African-American gospel spiritual: "Rock-A-My Soul", where the lyrics are sung repeatedly: "Rock-a-my soul in bosom of Abraham". I thought this was a particularly good analogy for the lesson. The passage speaks of God's promise to Abraham by an oath that "surely" guarantees *future blessings*; as well as *grace* upon those in Christ, who seek Him out in sacrificial service by becoming a "servant" entitled to share in the "inheritance".

Hebrews: 6:13-15

> For when God made his promise to Abraham, since he could swear by none greater, he swore by himself, saying: Surely blessing I will bless thee and multiplying I will multiply thee. And thus, having patiently endured (longsuffering) he obtained the promise. [18] (RV)

Christ is the *anchor*. What connects a Promise Seeking Christian to the promises are the *action steps*. Thus by analogy it is the hawser, or what one may call, the **Rope of Hope**. Being in need of an "R", repentance came to mind. Forgiveness is a necessity, for Christ said if you do not forgive others of their sins against you, I will not forgive you of your sins. An important part of repenting of one's sins is to forgive others. After this, the action words for hope came quickly.

To inherit the promises of God one must be tethered to the anchor of Jesus, so the rock of his soul is secure in the bosom of Abraham.

These action steps in this tethering are like building a strong rope from many strands, where each action step is another strand. Once I visited an old restored "rope house" at the Mystic Seaport Museum in Mystic Seaport, Connecticut. The large hawsers used on old sailing ships started with very small strands of fiber that were twisted together. These twisted strands were then themselves twisted or woven into larger strands, that were then again overlaid and twisted again to produce a large, very strong rope to which a heavy anchor could be attached. The spiritual action steps that a Promise Seeking Christian must take if they wish to tether Jesus securely to their ship are progressive. As in a large rope, some of the strongest, most important elements are found inside.

In his sermon "The Certainty of God's Promises", pastor Andrew Paton spoke to God's Oath being realized in Hebrews: 6:13-15. Andrew said: "We are speaking here about the Proof of God's Promise. If anyone needs proof that God can promise you something, we have it in the story of the life of Abraham. He *grew* in his relationship with God – he *grew* to the point where he could receive God's promise." Pastor Andrew elaborated further: "The first step in realizing the certainty of God's promises is that the promise must be *vocalized*." After reading Hebrews 6:13 & 14 aloud, pastor Andrew went on to explain: "One of the fruits of Christian maturity is the ability to *hear God*. Not with the ears but with your spirit. God, who is Spirit, will speak deep into your human spirit. So, do you have, what some might call, *'a polished ear'*?" [19]

*Clearly, the first and most important action step, or deep strand in our spiritual hawser, must be having a **Spirit to Hear** God's messages for each of us as individuals, or hearing His gentle leadings of Spirit, as some might say.*

29

Second, it is evident from Hebrews Chapter 11 that hearing a message from the Holy Spirit is of little use in glorifying God unless one *acts on Faith* by doing what the message reveals. Hebrews 11:1 exclaims, "Now faith is the assurance of things hoped for [in heaven], the conviction of things not seen [in heaven]." (NASB) Further, in Hebrews 11:6, the writer states, "And without faith it is impossible to please Him, for he who comes to God must believe that He is, and that He is a rewarder of those who seek Him." (NASB)

So, the second important action step, a deep fiber in our **Rope of Hope**, *is having* **Faith to Act** *on His will.*

Building this spiritual *hawser of hope* that will tether us to Jesus does, in-and-of-itself, involve considerable action on our part. One can choose, without any loss of salvation, to remain in the safe port of a community of Christians, tied to the dock (of a local church) by the human relationships of Christian friends, while the anchor of Jesus rests safely, without a hawser, on their ship's deck. But others, who choose to adventure the dynamic experience of Christ out on the stormy seas of an evil world, will first best build their holy *hawser of hope* large, long, and strong before setting sail.

A friend, who has sailed the globe for some 12 years, recently explained to me that this hawser anchor rope is not just used to connect the heavy metal anchor to the bottom of a sea while near land, but, also, it is used to secure a sea anchor during storms. A sea anchor is a large parachute that is connected to the end of the hawser and let out to sea during a storm. He said that the strong wind, sometimes 50 knots, pushes the ship on the surface that pulls the parachute anchor against the seas ahead of the ship. This disrupts the coming waves in a way that they do not break over the ship. In a storm, the sea anchor creates calm seas immediately around a ship. Without the sea anchor parachute on a long, strong hawser, the ship would be broken apart by the pounding waves of a storm. The same is true with our *hawser of hope*. In the storms of life in an evil world, Christ is also the sea anchor held firm by our *hawser of hope*. We rest calm and at peace amidst the storm with the promises of God secure in our hearts.

Coming back to pastor Andrew's sermon, he next asked the question: "Are you holding in your heart promises from God?" He explained: "You can see from what I just said that it's not enough to be a reader of the many promises of God right here in the Bible (the promises are vocalized there), but the promises must also be internalized." Repeating Scripture he read, "And so after waiting patiently, Abraham received what was promised." He went on to explain the important point that the key is to wait patiently on God: "The Word of God needs to find root in your heart. It takes a while for roots to grow. So, I give you a useful tool this morning: It's called – Meditating on God's Promises. You will find they internalize more quickly when you take time to mediate on them. The most basic form of meditation is to 'mutter under your breath.' Imagine what will become of you if people catch you muttering the promises of God under your breath. You will find that discovering Jesus to be a mighty Deliverer is dependent on the Proof of God's Promises." [20]

This leads to the third strand in our spiritual tether to Jesus, having **Patience to Wait** *for His blessings and grace.*

Do we really know what it means to wait? Ask any youngster in Japan, and you will learn a lesson of waiting from Japan's most famous dog, Hachiko. Hachi, as he was called, is of the rare Akita breed. At the time of the story, there were only thirty such canines known in Japan. Hachi's master, professor Hidesamuro Ueno, would leave his loyal companion sitting on his doorstep each morning as he traveled by train to work at the University of Tokyo. Hachi, who was free to roam, would be waiting at the Shibuya train station each day, a short time before professor Ueno's train arrived, so they could walk home together. One tragic day, Ueno died of a stroke while at work, and he never returned home. Hachi, however, continued to wait the return of his master everyday, at the same time and in the same spot, for ten years until he died. What Hachi did during his days is unknown, but at four o'clock each day for a decade, he would greet passengers at the Shibuya station, as he loyally waited for his master. Today, a bronze statue of Hachi stands at the Shibuya station, where he waited each day. Several films have been made about Hachi's loyal devotion.

The bond of sacrificial love between master and servant can be so strong that the servant returns day after day to wait upon his master in silent dedication.

Developing the **Patience to Wait** can build one's spiritual strength. Scripture to this effect is immortalized in the book of Isaiah, where it is written:

Isaiah 40:28-31

> Do you not know? Have you not heard? The everlasting God, the Lord, the Creator of the ends of the earth does not become weary or tired. His understanding is inscrutable. He gives strength to the weary, and to him who lacks might He increases power. Though youths grow weary and tired, and vigorous young men stumble badly, yet those who wait for the Lord will gain new strength: they will mount up with wings like eagles, they will run and not get tired, they will walk and not become weary. (NASB)

It is often said that God's time is not our time. One does not need to be overly anxious, for God shall surely reveal His will to every Promise Seeking believer in due time. It is better that one spends his time while waiting, building spiritual strength, sharpening his mind, softening his heart, and preparing himself for the tasks ahead.

T. C. PINKERTON

Moving on to the fourth strand, as we saw in Lesson 3, the life of a Promise Seeking Christian is most distinguished by their willingness to sacrifice themselves for the good and care of others. This brings to mind Luke 9:23.

Luke 9:23

> And He was saying to them all, "If anyone wishes to come after Me, let him deny himself, and take up his cross daily, and follow Me." (NASB)

Fully denying oneself by giving up on one's own desires, priorities, and plans; in exchange for utilizing one's time, resources, talents, and strength to care for others is a distinctive mark of a Promise Seeking Christian. The fact that Jesus called on his followers to do this "daily" is a reaffirmation of the point made in Lesson 3 that Promise Seeking Christians are primarily to work out their Faith every day *in their personal lives*, not necessarily in local religious organizations.

*This brings us to the fourth fiber in our hawser of hope, having **Courage to Sacrifice** by denying self, taking up one's cross daily, and following Jesus by doing "what is right" in the sight of God in all circumstances.*

In his book *The Holiest of All,* Andrew Murray says: "The Christian life is a race. To begin profits nothing unless we run to the end and reach the goal. Faith may accept, but only longsuffering inherits the promise." [21] Elaborating further Murray exclaims: "The church of Christ is a very hospital of backsliding Christians, who meant honestly, in the joy of their first love, to live wholly for God, and who yet gradually sank down into a life of formality and feebleness. There is nothing the church needs more than the preaching of daily diligence and perseverance as the indispensable condition of growth and strength. Let us learn from the epistle how these virtues can be fostered in ourselves and others." Later on Murray makes the cost of the inheriting servant crystal clear when he says: "Remember it is not easy to receive and claim this promise. Abraham received it in the way of faith and obedience and self-sacrifice, in the entire surrender to God's will and leading." [22]

*The fifth trait overlays the already interwoven underlying strands in the growing holy hawser of hope, when one realizes the extraordinary need of having **Perseverance to Endure** one's self-sacrifice in an evil world of abuse. This attribute needs no explanation.*

Mature Christians know it from experience, as well as from the blunt proclamation in Hebrews 10:36:

Hebrews 10:36

> For you have need of endurance, so that when you have done the will of God, you may receive what was promised. (NASB)

In history, kind masters have been known to treat selected servants well, but the world around them still treats them like servants. As such, servants in a hateful world often had to *endure* condescension, humiliation, insults, belittlement, mockery, drudgery, boredom, confinement, and self-denial in their positions of service. One must take to heart what Jesus meant when he said, "If the world hates you, you know that it hated me first." (John 15:18, Phillips). The "self-sacrifice" of which the Scripture speaks for a Promise Seeking Christian is not the benevolent service among the comfortable, self-assuring, supportive friends of a local religious organization; but the self-sacrificing commitment in one's personal life doing "what is right" in an abusive world.

One of the best depictions of what the Scripture means by this courage to self-sacrifice with perseverance to endure in an evil world is Frank Capra's movie: "It's A Wonderful Life". For many Christmas seasons this film has been viewed, over and over again, by millions of people for half a century, because its spiritual truth is recognized by so many. George Bailey, who does not seem to have much of a life, remains trapped in a small town, while others go off to realize their dreams and adventures. George, on the other hand, each time he reaches a critical cross-road in life that might lead him out of Bedford Falls to his worldly dreams, is confronted with a decision that means: if he does "what is right" in the sight of God to stand up against the evil of the day, represented by Potter's desire to control the town, he will need to give up his dreams – one more time – and sacrifice himself, his money, and his future. His fight against the wrongs of this world seem hopeless, as every pursuit does not work out, because of circumstances beyond his control. He finally plans to end his life, for he feels it would have been better had he "never been born". Then his guardian angel, Clarence, comes to give him a rare privilege: to see what the world would have been like without him. He is able to see, first hand, what the Scripture means by how one's life is touched by so many. Others are blessed by these inner connections and by the decisions of those who choose to sacrifice themselves, in order to become servants by doing Godly good in standing up against an evil world.

By being genuinely godlike in these critical crossroad decisions of life, the Promise Seeking Christian blesses others; and the blessed then choose to bless others, as well. The blessings are multiplied over and over as others join in by making similar godlike self-sacrifices. In the absence of such sacrifice, as captured so well in the film "It's A Wonderful Life", people become more selfish, more self-absorbed, and more self-pleasing; they become a part of the decadent world around them, which sinks further into degradation and decay.

Andrew Murray speaks of Abraham's "heart of confidence that the blessing was indeed to be something very wonderful and worthy of God, blessing in divine power and fullness." Repeating the lesson in Hebrews: "Multiplying I will multiply thee", Murray says that "scripture teaches us that the highest blessing God can bestow, what makes us truly godlike, is the power of multiplying ourselves – of becoming, as God is, the source and the blessing of other lives." Quoting Genesis 1:22, 1:28 and 9:1, Murray goes on to strengthen the point by saying: "It is the glory of God that He is the Dispenser of life – that in His creatures He multiplies His own life and blessedness." [23]

Anyone with eyes to see and a "spiritual ear to hear" knows this multiplying of blessings through "divine power and fullness" of the Holy Spirit. They know this happens by the dispensing of a self-sacrificing life of George Bailey's type of godlike blessed hope to those whom one's life crosses. A self-sacrificing focus blesses; whereas, a self-satisfying focus transgresses. Murray goes on to say that, "Every believer who will but claim and give himself up to the blessing of God will find that the blessing is a power of the divine life that will make him fruitful in blessing to others." ... "Even we, like Christ, can become priests, bringing the blessing of God to those who know Him not." Murray hangs on this point of deep paradoxical understanding when he drives home the message: "It is when this fullness of blessing in its divine energy – when this *'blessing I will bless thee'* begins to be understood and the soul sees that there is something beyond the mere being saved from wrath – that the soul becomes the *recipient*, the *channel*, and the *dispenser of life* and *blessing to others*. It becomes willing to sacrifice everything and, in longsuffering, to *endure* until it obtains the promise." [24]

Murray now challenges each individual who wishes to become a Promise Seeking believer: "Christians, would you be an imitator of Abraham and let the God who spoke to him speak to you? Remember it is not so easy to receive and claim the promise. Abraham received it in the way of *faith* and *obedience* and *self-sacrifice*, in the entire surrender to God's will and leading." [25]

Last but not least, the sixth fiber in this hawser of hope is having the wherewithal to seek out and act on **Forgiveness to Repent** *by His saving grace.*

This final very necessary action is quite clearly pronounced by Jesus in Matthew 6:14-15 when he said: "For if you forgive men for their transgressions, your heavenly Father will also forgive you. But if you do not forgive men, then your Father will not forgive your transgressions." (NASB) Equally, John in Revelation 3:19 encourages believers to not sit idly by and neglect the importance of seeking out proactively the *forgiveness* through *repentance* when he brought forth God's message to the church in Laodicea, "All those whom I love I *correct* and *discipline*; therefore, shake off your complacency and *repent*." (Phillips)

Now, with this *hawser of hope* firmly anchoring the Promise of God through Christ to one's soul, a Promise Seeking believer can strive to hoist in the blessings for others by taking on their daily, individual *responsibility*

to **H**ear – **A**ct – **W**ait – **S**acrifice – **E**ndure – **R**epent; thus empting self

by surrendering and giving up on those quests for worldly satisfaction, which motivate one to make ungodly decisions at life's critical crossroads. Having strived to empty one of SELF by giving over to the Holy Spirit, or Christ within, one mysteriously encounters a filling of the blessings that bless others.

This paradox of being filled by God through the emptying of one's SELF,

- brings on joy to **H**ope in the rewards of heaven,
- the diligence to **O**bey by abiding in the Word, and
- the discipline to **P**ray fervently in all things, which leads
- to a trust in the **E**ternal.

This in turn enables one to hold fast until the end of one's journey as a stranger in this world and to be ushered into one's inheritance of the Promise. In all of this, one must not forget Murray's convicting words, when he said, "*Remember it is not easy to receive and claim the promise.*" Meaning, the degree of our participation and inheritance in the Promise will be in proportion to the Hearing, Acting, Waiting, Sacrificing, Enduring, and Repenting we do on this earth. One needs to look into the reflection of the soul and ask: Have I had "A Wonderful Life"?

One might ask themselves

- Have my life decisions taken me closer or farther away from God?
- Have I sacrificed my time and resources to provide for my family?
- Have I cared for a family member in need?
- Have I been completely honest and ethical in all my dealings?
- Have I defended "what is right" in the eyes of God to my disadvantage?
- Have I risked my life, my future plans, or my finances to help another?
- Have I prayed fervently for others and seen those prayers fulfilled?

If not, you might ask yourself: What should I do to inherit the Promise?

Truly on earth, everyone IS created equal in the sight of God, but in eternity, one will have become the person in this life he so CHOSE to be.

The H A W S E R of H O P E is

1.	having <u>Spirit</u>	to **H**ear – His message,
2.	having <u>Faith</u>	to **A**ct – on His will,
3.	having <u>Patience</u>	to **W**ait – for His blessings and grace,
4.	having <u>Courage</u>	to **S**acrifice – by taking up one's cross daily,
5.	having <u>Perseverance</u>	to **E**ndure – in an evil world,
6.	having <u>Forgiveness</u>	to **R**epent – by His saving grace,

of

7.	having <u>Joy</u>	to **H**ope – in the rewards of heaven,
8.	having <u>Diligence</u>	to **O**bey – by abiding in the Word,
9.	having <u>Discipline</u>	to **P**ray – fervently in all things
10.	having <u>Trust</u> leads	to **E**ternal hope, thus holding fast to the end.

Reiterating, the *hawser of hope* anchors one's soul to God's promises through Christ, who today sits next to God on the throne as the High Priest of Heaven, dynamically acting on behalf of believers when they seek His assistance in helping others. (Hebrews 6:19-20)

Group Discussion

The Life Group discussion focused on *surrendering* oneself and being thankful for what God has made available to us by His grace. The questions, in the minds of some, were about mental burdens that one might have difficulty releasing.

Why do we hold on to mental burdens that hold us back and inhibit us from making spiritual progress towards realizing the promises of God?

In His first commandment, Jesus said that we must love the Lord thy God with *all* our heart, mind, soul, and strength. Without enabling this first commandment, one cannot move on fully to the second or third commandment. Each of these entities represents a part of the human being. The heart is the center of ones desires and motivations. One's mind is the primary functioning tool that controls the body. The soul is the spiritual center, where morality and the Holy Spirit reside. The strength relates to each of these entities but brings in the physical body, as well. The body is the temple – or vessel – of God within which Christ's Spirit lives. As such, one must consider what stands in the way of one's whole being functioning as a Spirit-filled Christian? What prevents one from striving to become "perfect" in Christ?

Many people have particular ills of the heart, mind, soul, and body. If deep in one's motivational center (i.e., one's "heart of hearts"), a person holds onto worldly desires, so as to satisfy some perceived necessary fulfillment of a self-defined purpose; or, if one is psychologically burdened with a hurt from childhood, adolescence, or adulthood, and these thoughts linger in the mind; or, if one feels an emptiness for having done little to genuinely build a moral character; or, if one is obsessed or preoccupied with not just caring for or preserving the body, but admonishing it continually with undue attention; then, one needs to consider whether they are remaining in a state of worldly spiritual illness or immaturity, thus being unable to receive the blessings from God.

Paul spoke to this inability to receive gifts from God, owing to one's lack of spiritual maturity in Ephesians 4:12-16, and again in the oft read, but little practiced, verses in I Corinthians Chapter 13.

Ephesians 4:12-16

> His gifts were made that Christians might be properly equipped for their service, that the whole body might be built up until the time comes when, in the unity of common faith and common knowledge of the Son of God, we arrive at a *real maturity* – that measure of development which is meant by 'fullness of Christ'. We are *not meant to remain as children* at the mercy of every chance wind of teaching, and of the jockeying of men who are expert in the crafty presentation of lies. But we are meant to speak the truth in love, and to *grow up in every way* into Christ, the head. For it is from the head that the whole body, as a harmonious structure knit together by the joints with which it is provided, grows by the proper functioning of individual parts, and so builds itself up in love. [26]

It is unfortunate that the "whole body" is too often misinterpreted as being only those who work for religious organizations. This "unity of common faith and common knowledge" is incorrectly assumed to be the larger unification of many smaller religious organizations within a larger denominational infrastructure, thus forming a "harmonious" unity of believers. Down through history, anyone with eyes to see knows that religious organizations are anything but unified and even less harmonious. No, the "body of Christ", so noted by Paul, is the mysterious, unseen collection of mature believers out in the world casting God's blessings on unsuspecting recipients through acts of God's *agape* love. As in Frank Capra's "It's A Wonderful Life", where the believers were unified by unseen threads of kindness, so invisible that George Bailey, the benevolent seamster, could not even understand that he had spent his whole life weaving together such loving acts of generosity.

The Apostle Paul goes on speaking to this spiritual coming-of-age growth and definition of God's *agape* love, when he says:

I Corinthians 13:11-13

> When I was a little child [i.e., meaning spiritually immature] I talked and felt and thought like a little child [i.e., like a spiritually immature, worldly person]. Now that I am a man [i.e., having accepted God with a mature mind], I have finished with childish things [i.e., done with the worldly desires of my feelings]. At present we are men looking at puzzling reflections in a mirror [i.e., wondering why we cannot grow in our Faith]. The time will come when we shall see reality whole and face to face! [i.e., when we are confronted with the reality of God and the struggle of good and evil in this world] At present all I know is a little fraction of the truth, but the time will come when I shall know it as fully as God has known me! In this life we have three lasting qualities – *faith*, *hope*, and *love*. But the greatest of them is *love*. [27] [text inserted by author, not translator]

I Corinthians 13:4-8

> This *love* of which I speak is slow to lose patience – it looks for a way of being constructive. It is not possessive, it is neither anxious to impress nor does it cherish inflated ideas of its own importance. Love has good manners and does not pursue selfish advantage. It is not touchy. It does not keep account of evil or gloat over the wickedness of other people. On the contrary, it shares the joy of those who live by the truth. Love knows no limit to its *endurance*, no end to its *trust*, no fading of its *hope*; it can outlast anything. Love never fails. [28]

After Paul recorded this reflective transition of one's growth from being spiritually immature to mature in Faith and the definition of God's *agape* love, called for by Christ's third commandment to sacrifice oneself, he makes a strong declaration in the next chapter, when he says:

I Corinthians 14:20

> My brothers, don't be children but *use your intelligence*! By all means be innocent as babes as far as evil is concerned, but where your *minds* are concerned be *full-grown* men! [29]

Since one's mind is the functioning element that communicates everything from one's heart and soul into actions of the body, it is key that the mind be healed of any psychological wounds. It cannot be explained how God can heal the mind of an individual through the sacrificial atonement of Christ's dying on the cross, but there are countless examples of this very thing happening to people, over and over again, down through history.

Although oversimplified, one might think that "wounds" of the mind are brought on by some evil act of another person, and it is the persistent thought of this injustice, or of being unfairly treated, in the mind of an individual, that holds power over him. A worldly need to seek justice, to get revenge, or to right the wrong eats away at a person like a slow growing cancer that starts with one small cell until it consumes the entire body. One needs to understand that Jesus, who walked the earth in his brief thirty years, was morally perfect, having never sinned; but He was executed in a most cruel manner for simply bringing to light and disseminating the knowledge of God. Jesus, of all people, was given the greatest injustice; yet He voluntarily accepted the sacrifice of His life without appealing to the authority figure present who wanted to free him. Once one comes to grips with this realization, the "wounds" of the mind, which seem so trivial by comparison, melt away into fresh water like ice in a shining sun. Anyone who has experienced this healing of the mind is awestruck to put the experience into words, but they know it happened by the grace of God and that it made them "whole" again.

Alex spoke to this phenomenon when he enumerated that we must first give *praise* to God for our complete healing at the cross. Then, we must *trust* God and *accept* such healings of Christ's work on the cross by grace, as a free gift. Finally, we must give thanks to God for what He has "already done".

Often those of Faith fail to understand that much of the "healing" work, for which they seek, is already done. It is more a matter of releasing one's grip mentally on the worldly desire for justice, recompense, and revenge. That release frees one from the psychological burdens. This frees one to use his "intelligence" with a "full-grown" mind to conceive of how one might sacrifice himself in the service of others with God's *agape* love. In fact, for one to grow-up into having "A Wonderful Life".

The discussion continued with a focus on the slow *surrendering* of oneself to God. The group reflected on testimonies where people, who experienced difficult circumstances involving "longsuffering", conveyed a need to "off-load" worldly baggage as a part of the surrendering process to grow closer to God.

In life, every individual encounters difficult situations, struggles, and tragedies. How one responds to these circumstances determines whether one grows closer to God or drifts farther away. One can become angry, bitter, and resentful; or one can become more calm, composed, and constructive. It is one's own choice. A person can attempt to escape and avoid the psychological impact of a hardship, or he can choose to go through it with forthright mental courage.

A Christian who desires to grow in Faith will view "longsuffering" as an opportunity to strengthen his character by humbling himself before God. A genuine believer tends to identify a character trait that is standing in the way of his spiritual growth. These worldly traits are seen as unnecessary "baggage" one must "off-load" in order to become more mature in Faith.

Jesus said: "It is easier for a camel to go through the eye of a needle than for a rich man to enter the kingdom of God." Mark 10:25 (NASB) In that time, strong ropes were often made of camel hair, so Jesus was not referring to the animal itself, but the large difficult to unravel rope, which carried its nickname. The aphorism means that one cannot take his love for worldliness into heaven, and one cannot grow spiritually on earth if he holds onto worldly behavior.

Off-loading inappropriate "baggage" might be realized when

- one stops doubting and starts trusting God more fully, or when
- one stops complaining and starts being thankful in all things, or when
- one stops blaming and starts accepting responsibility for actions, or when
- one stops criticizing and starts encouraging others, or when
- one stops manipulating and starts cooperating constructively, or when
- one stops controlling and starts being helpful.

In essence, when one lets go of the final vestiges of being a "TAKER" and starts wholeheartedly embracing the role of becoming a "GIVER"; then, and only then, does one begin to move along a path towards true spiritual maturity.

Jesus said, "For the gate is small and the way is narrow that leads to life, and few are those who find it." Matthew 7:14 (NASB) During a "trial by fire", a believer often views his path amidst "longsuffering" as small narrow openings through which he must pass to grow closer to God. The problem is that his worldly "baggage" will not fit through these narrow passageways. He concludes he must give up some immature character traits so as to become a more Godly person.

Once one begins to "off-load" these, and other, selfish character traits, as he passes through each narrowing gate of annealing fire; he surprisingly discovers a filling of the Holy Spirit and the accompanying fruits of the Spirit with its inner blessings.

Three times during the discussion, the Life Group came back to Andrew Murray's profound, sobering wisdom: "When this *'blessing I will bless thee'* begins to be understood and the soul sees that there is something beyond the mere being saved from wrath – that the soul becomes the recipient, the channel, and the dispenser of life and blessings to others".

It is a perplexing paradox, most difficult for a human being to understand, that consciously *emptying* oneself of worldly desires, genuinely for Christ's sake to give glory to God, either voluntarily or by virtue of difficult circumstances, leads one, surprisingly, to be *filled* with a "power of the divine life" that makes one "fruitful in blessing others". Of course, no one can fool God, so without genuine, wholehearted, self-sacrificing love and care for others, such filling with a "divine life" of spiritual blessings does not happen. Those who have experienced such filling, however, are well aware of the paradox. They can look back over their lives and see the times when the "power of the divine life" expressed itself and those times of personal regression, when such divine blessings were inherently, almost automatically, attenuated. Giving up oneself, without a desire for a reward in this world, is a most difficult concept for a person to grasp and hold onto. A focus on the eternal is necessary. Several passages in Matthew were brought to the minds of Life Group members. Jesus said:

Matthew 5:16

> "Let your light shine before men in such a way that they may see your good works, and glorify your Father who is in heaven." (NASB)

Matthew 10:38-39

> "And he who does not take his cross and follow Me is not worthy of Me. He who has found his life shall lose it, and he who has lost his life for My sake shall find it." (NASB)

The Promise Seeking Christian, who has genuinely "lost his life" by off-loading his worldly "baggage" of desires so he can make it through these ever narrowing Spiritual doors of discipline, will "*find* his life" for Christ's sake; with the filling of blessings that can bless others through "longsuffering" self-sacrifice.

This was a sobering message for the Life Group. A few members were not so eager to embrace the lesson. Others in the group, who had already experienced "longsuffering", and the corresponding "power of the divine life", could see its truth; but they were not so willing to embark on another such journey. Equally, they remained a bit reticent to encourage others to do the same. Such journeys require a very mature, disciplined, personal commitment of Faith. It is evident that a very wholehearted motivation is a prerequisite and a genuine "calling" from God to pick-up one's cross is necessary, before embarking on such a self-sacrificing spiritual journey.

Knowing that most of the Life Group members were very seasoned Christians, I asked if anyone wanted to share their "longsuffering" experience that might have transitioned them from being a Salvation Satisfied to a Promise Seeking believer. No one volunteered to share. This is most likely because such experiences are extremely personal, and humility dictates caution. Since no one volunteered, I decided to tell the story of my mother's such experience.

T. C. PINKERTON

My mother grew up in a Christian home. Her grandfather, her mother's father, was a minister. When she was young they attended her grandfather's church, and he baptized her as a youth. The whole family was well versed in the Bible. After her father passed away, when I was too young to remember, my grandmother began teaching Bible at a private school for boys, which she did for some years. My mother was a model Christian. We went to church every Sunday. We all participated in church activities; we read the Bible and prayed at home. My mother, however, had visions of her life in a Southern culture. When I was very young, my father purchased a large, old frame house, for which I have very fond memories. As an architect and an accomplished artist, he demonstrated his talents by restoring the old house to its original grandeur. My mother was very formal. Each Sunday the roast cooked while we attended church. Arriving home, still in our suits, ties, and uncomfortable shoes, my two brothers and I went about our duties of setting the white lace covered long dining table with sterling silver, ornate dishes, antique goblets, and linen napkins. We were properly trained in the etiquette of the day, and we were expected, with fear of stern discipline in our hearts, to behave like "little gentlemen". My mother was enormously respected in the community. She was president of the Women's Club, chairperson of my elementary school PTA, and organizer of local cultural events. Some card party or social gathering was always transpiring at our house. As a Boy Scout Master and local artist, my father was equally involved in the community. Although religion was an integral part of our lives during the 1950s in Kentucky, it seemed more akin to the culture around us than to personal conviction.

In this idyllic Southern lifestyle, one's reputation seemed to be more a driver of motivation to be an accepted member of society than holding to one's internal beliefs. When I was twelve years old everything changed. My father, whose architectural expertise was designing hospitals, did not see career growth potential in a small town, so we moved across the state to a large city. There he was able to join a large firm and head up the design of the state's largest university medical complex. Our beloved old house, amongst the large oaks in a serene neighborhood of a peaceful town, was quickly sold; and we moved into a small rented house in closely packed rows on a busy street next to shopping in the city. The shock to all of us was enormous. My mother's community involvement was gone, and family friends disappeared. I rarely saw my father anymore, as he often worked late. After the medical complex was finished, his work in the firm focused mainly on banks, schools, and drawing artist renderings. Being dissatisfied with the firm, he decided to start his own business. He was an extremely talented artist and architect, but, being too generous, he was not a good businessman. We stayed longer than expected in the depressing little rented house on the busy street, and my mother had to go to work full-time as a secretary for us to survive.

Then came the tragic news that my father was diagnosed with cancer. As he underwent operations and chemotherapy, again and again, what little savings my parents had was gone. My mother continued to work as a secretary until I, being the youngest, graduated from college; whereupon, my parents moved to another state where my father, having given up on his business, could find work with a firm that provided full health benefits. My father survived with cancer for nine years until his death; during which time I observed my mother slowly transformed from a Salvation Satisfied Christian into a Promise Seeking Christian.

She gave up the socialite reputation of her Southern upbringing, the treasured possessions of her desires, and the visions of her worldly dreams. In the place of those worldly things came a gentle heart, a kindly manner, a listening ear, a patient perseverance, a spiritual wisdom, and a prayerful discipline. For over thirty years after my father's passing, she lived independently with a "power of the divine" as her life touched many. She taught water aerobics, became a writer of family history, served as spiritual counselor at a call-in center, sang in her church choir, helped many friends in need, and prayed endlessly for everyone. I could not honestly describe my mother to anyone without saying I knew two entirely different individuals. One was a very religiously strict, almost cold, but properly respected, upstanding proud pillar of the community; while the other was a warm, lovingly kind elegant lady of service to all she encountered. I prefer to remember her as the latter, rather than the former. The transition from Salvation Satisfied believer to Promise Seeking believer had transpired over the nine years of "longsuffering" as a care-giver to my father.

The question arose in the group: Can one become a Promise Seeking believer without experiencing "longsuffering"? No one really had the answer, as "God only knows". There were suggestions that perhaps voluntarily surrendering early in life might minimize "longsuffering" later in life. Attempting to avoid "longsuffering" might bring on tragic circumstances that could force the transition in an even more difficult way. It was noted that how far one chooses to progress along the journey to "become perfect" in Christ is solely up to the individual. Equally, one might wish to be careful for that which one prays, as it might very well come true. Knowing that God is more committed to us than we are to Him, a request will be fulfilled by God, if we abide in Him. It is instructive to remember, one more time, the story of the mother of the sons of Zebedee (James and John), who asked Jesus if her sons could sit by His side in heaven.

Matthew 20:20-28

> Then the mother of the sons of Zebedee came to Him with her sons, bowing down, and making a request of Him. And He said to her, "What do you wish?" She said to Him, "Command that in Your Kingdom these two sons of mine

may sit, one on Your right and one on Your left." But Jesus answered and said, "You do not know what you are asking, for are you able to drink the cup that I am about to drink?" They said to Him, "We are able." He said to them, "My cup you shall drink; but to sit on My right and on My left, this is not Mine to give, but it is for those for whom it has been prepared by My Father." And hearing this, the ten became indignant with the two brothers. But Jesus called them to Himself, and said, "You know that the rulers of the Gentiles' lord is over them, and their great men exercise authority over them. It is not among you, but whoever wishes to become great among you shall be your servant, and whoever wishes to be first among you must be your slave; just as the Son of Man did not come to be served, but to serve, and to give His life as a ransom for many." (NASB)

Jesus remonstrated her with the reply, "you do not know what you are asking"; for He knew the sons would need to follow after Him and experience His destiny. Jesus agreed, but she still did not realize the "longsuffering" that was to come to her two sons, because of her request. Perhaps voluntarily surrendering oneself to many periods of suffering where one becomes a "servant" or "slave" is easier to bear than one very long stretch of suffering. The question remains open. Christ said one would not be given more than he could bear.

Breathe on Me, Breath of God [30]
Edwin Hatch (1835-1889)

Breathe on me, Breath of God; Fill me with Life anew,
That I may love what Thou dost love, And do what Thou wouldst do.

Breathe on me, Breath of God, Until my heart is pure,
Until with Thee I will one will, To do and to endure.

Breathe on me, Breath of God, Till I am wholly Thine,
Until this earthly part of me, Glow with Thy fire divine

Breathe on me, Breath of God, so shall I never die,
But live with Thee the perfect life, Of Thine eternity.

Jesus: The High Priest in a Heavenly Sanctuary

Life Group Meetings in February 2013
Primary Scripture: Hebrews 6:16-20

By the Word and Oath of God

The last part of Hebrews Chapter 6 confirms the promises of God by two undeniable things: (i) the Word of God and (ii) the Oath of God. It summarizes what Andrew Murray calls "the central teaching of the epistle". Murray describes this critically significant theme when he says: "There are specifically two great heavenly mysteries that he [the author of Hebrews] was commissioned to unfold. The first is that of the *heavenly priesthood* of Christ; the second is that of the *heavenly sanctuary* in which He today ministers and into which *He gives us access.*" If a believer has the trust, faith, and endurance to follow Jesus into that heavenly sanctuary in the same manner He did, as the "*forerunner*" who opened the way for us by "Himself walking in it", that believer can inherit the promises of God. [31]

Hebrews 6:16-20

> Among men it is customary to swear by something greater than themselves. And if a statement is confirmed by an Oath, that is the end of the quibbling. So in this matter, God, wishing to show the heirs of his promise even more clearly that his plan was unchangeable, confirmed it with an oath. So that by two utterly immutable things, the word of God and the oath of God, who cannot lie, we who are refugees from this dying world might have a powerful source of strength, and might grasp the hope that he holds out for our souls, fixed in the innermost shrine of Heaven, where Jesus has already entered on our behalf, having become, as we have seen, High Priest forever "after the order of Melchizedek". [32]

So, where is Jesus Christ today, at this very moment? The author of Hebrews tells us that He is the eternal High Priest at the right hand of God in a heavenly sanctuary, where the Promise Seeking believer can enter into this "place" with Him, even while still on earth, and access the very power of the universe to do God's will. Entering into this heavenly sanctuary by "walking in Christ's footsteps", the "heirs of His promise" – dynamically in real-time – anchor their souls to Christ.

God is the father of all honesty and truth! Satan is the father of all lies and deception! God cannot tell a lie, and being the all powerful creator of the universe, He cannot give an oath by any other than Himself. The author wants the suffering Promise Seeking believers, who trust in God, to know that those who step out in Faith to do God's will, irrespective of what happens on earth in this life, can be assured that God will fulfill His promise to them. Every prayer will be answered, and every reward will be delivered; if not in this life, then in the next.

Andrew Murray puts it this way: "Here he [the author of Hebrews] wished to show believers what strong encouragement they have in God's oath to expect most confidently the fulfillment of the promise. It is this confidence *alone* that will enable the Christian to endure and conquer." [33] Murray goes on the explain: "The oath of God plainly proves that the thing He seeks above everything is *Faith*; He wishes to be *trusted. Faith* is nothing but depending on God to do for us what we cannot do – what He has undertaken to do. God's purpose concerning us is something of infinite and inconceivable blessedness. He is ready – He longs! – as God Himself *to work in us* all that He has promised." [34]

If the Promise Seeking believer opens his heart in humility to trust in the real-life practice of Godly decision-making, as commanded in His Word, and accepts the resulting consequences of "longsuffering" in patience, endurance, and perseverance; then this Faith will open his heart to a life of fulfilled expectations and hope. Once a believer has reached this point in his faith-walk in the real-world of everyday life, which is very much "outside the camp" of a comfortable, safe, and secure environment of a supportive religious community; then God can begin to do His most important work on the soul of this believer. Murray says at this point: "God is free to work; Faith gives Him His place as God, and it *honors* Him; and He fulfills the promise, 'them that honor me I will honor' (1 Samuel 2:30 RV). Oh, do learn the lesson of the first and the last – the one thing – God asks is that we *trust* Him to do His work." [35]

Strong Encouragement for Disciplined Believers

This work of God on the Promise Seeking believer's soul generally follows periods of undeserved "longsuffering". The believer, through prayerful listening, faith-based actions, and diligent perseverance in humility, has chosen to prepare himself for this work of God by doing what is necessary on his part to "open the heart". The believer being sufficiently prepared, God can do with his Faith what the believer cannot do for himself. It becomes quite significant and important for the believer to discern and to understand clearly what "he" can do for himself, and what God will do by His grace, as promised. Reiterating Faith as defined by Murray: *"Faith is nothing but depending on God to do for us what we cannot do."* Of course, the great definition of Faith is found in Hebrews Chapter 11.

Hebrews 11:1

> Now faith means that we have full confidence in the things we hope for; it means being certain of things we cannot see. [36]

Faith, by its very nature, may be blind, but it is certainly not imperceptive. The Promise Seeking believer can "hear" God's direction by listening with "a polished ear", and the believer may use – to his best abilities – his God given intelligence, knowledge, and wisdom to do those things he is expected by God to do for himself. Murray puts it this way when he says: "In the Christian life, there is lack of steadfastness, of diligence, of perseverance. Of all, the cause is simply this – lack of faith. And of this again, the cause is simply this – lack of the knowledge of what God *wills* and *is*: of His purpose and His power to bless most wonderfully: and of His faithfulness to carry out His purpose." [37] So, what does the Promise Seeking believer need above all else? The answer is in Hebrew 10:36.

Hebrews 10:36

> Patient *endurance* is what you need if, after doing God's will, you are to receive what he has promised. [38]

Of course, the lack of knowing "what God *wills* and *is*" rests with the believer's genuine quest to *understand* and to *know* primarily God's message in the New Testament and to accept the Holy Spirit *within* himself as a real guide and teacher.

It is disappointing that many Salvation Satisfied Christians, who may "show off" the magnitude of the Bible they have memorized, often have much less of an understanding and recall of the meaning of what they so proudly recite. Diligence in understanding, discerning, and knowing the meaning of Scripture should be a higher priority than memorization. Once one *knows* who God "is" and what he "wills" for the believer, then taking real action on Faith leads one to the "longsuffering", where "patient endurance" is required to receive that which is promised.

During these times of trial, the Promise Seeking believer might ask: Have I done everything I am supposed to do? The previous lessons have explored many of the things a Promise Seeking believer is expected to do. (see Table I in Lesson 3 and the *Hawser of Hope* in Lesson 4). One might ask the following questions:

- Have I been completely honest with myself and others?
- Have I cared for those closest to me with self-sacrificing love?
- Have I been diligent in prayer for others' needs?
- Have I honored God with my behavior, speech, and action?
- Have I forgiven others?
- Have I asked God for forgiveness of my transgressions and omissions?
- Have I checked whether my motives were genuine in faith-action steps?
- Have I been abiding by doing His will or have I been sidetracked?
- Have I developed my gifts and talents to the fullest?
- Have I been generous with my time, talents, and resources?
- Have I let go of the past with its unnecessary burdens?
- Have I freed myself from any religious myths or cultural rituals?
- Have I "grasped that purpose for which Christ Jesus has grasped me"? [39]
- Have I been living a disciplined life?
- Have I worked at my job or career to the fullest of my potential?

As Paul said to the Philippians, "I forget all that lies behind me and with hands outstretched to whatever lies ahead I go straight for the goal – my reward the honor of my high calling by God in Christ Jesus." [40]

Often the last point in this list is overlooked. If believers incorrectly assume that God will "simply just take care of everything", because the Bible says He will "meet our every need"; then they may live in disappointment and struggle when meeting their physical needs in a very real world (see Murray's comments in Lesson 1). Christ probably meant that God was more interested in meeting one's more important spiritual needs than one's physical wants and desires. For that which one can do for themselves – physical needs and wants – are primarily the responsibility of the believer.

Paul made this point distinctively evident in his second letter to the Christians at Thessalonica, who had become so enthralled with the presumed impending coming of Christ in their time, that they had quit working for a living. Paul spends most of the last chapter delivering a very stern warning that it was quite unacceptable for Christians to live undisciplined lives, and that the food they eat should be earned by themselves. Paul refers to his own example while he was with them; reminding them that he worked day and night at his own trade, so he would not have to ask them for food. He states a biblical edict regarding work that says: *"If a man will not work, he shall not eat."* (II Thessalonians 3:10) Those wishing to become Promise Seeking believers should not take this warning lightly. Regarding physical needs and wants, Promise Seeking believers should become as independent, self-supporting, and self-reliant as their talents and abilities will allow. They should not expect God to do for them what He clearly expects them to do for themselves.

A Powerful Source of Innermost Strength

Next, the author of Hebrews makes an extremely profound proclamation: Each Promise Seeking believer has at their disposal – dynamically in real-time – the living Christ in a heavenly shrine "as a powerful source of strength" ready to bless. If the believer has the courage to step out in Faith and apply the commandments that Christ first demonstrated as the "forerunner", during His short life on earth, then a significant transformation will take place in that believer. Experiencing this innermost strength as an indwelling of the Holy Spirit equips the Promise Seeking believer with a reliable hope that anchors one's soul directly to Christ in heaven, who is the eternal High Priest at God's right hand, dispensing blessings according to God's will.

Andrew Murray notes that the author felt the Hebrew Christians, to which he was speaking, were "too far back in the Christian life to be able to receive this higher teaching." [41] This being the case, he was ready to address the most important "central teaching of the epistle" for which he was "commissioned to unfold" and reveal "two great heavenly mysteries." [42] The first is *Christ's heavenly priesthood* as the eternal High Priest, and the second is *His heavenly sanctuary* into which He invites the Promise Seeking believer to join Him in His administration of God's resources to do God's will. For these Hebrew Christians, access to this sanctuary with Christ in the heavenly Holiest of Holies must have been an extremely unthinkable and unheard of revelation. They must have asked themselves: Can an individual believer while still on earth enter into heaven today – dynamically in real-time – and access through Christ the power of God to do His will by way of the Holy Spirit? It must have been as profound a moment as when Nicodemus was perplexed by Jesus' revelation of how one must be "born-again" in the Spirit to know God and enter heaven. Remember Jesus' reply to Nicodemus was that if he could not even understand what happened on earth, how could he possibly begin to understand what goes on in heaven.

Murray says it this way: "The access to our High Priest in heaven gives [or puts] us into God's very presence, into the enjoyment of His fellowship and blessedness, even while we are here on earth renders to the believer an assured hope. He wisely acclaims, 'Where our hope lives, there the heart lives. There we, our real selves, are living, too.' " [43]

REALIZING THE PROMISES OF GOD

Murray believes a key point to this epistle is that Christ opened the way for all believers to have an indwelling of the Holy Spirit by Himself walking in the way of God as the "forerunner". The old King James version reads, "Whither as a forerunner Jesus entered for us" (Hebrews 6:20). The word whither means "to what place, result, or condition" shall one go. [44] "Whither thou goest, I will go." (Ruth 1:16, KJV). The inference here is quite strong. It means that if a Promise Seeking believer wants to enter into the heavenly sanctuary with Christ, then the believer must walk in Christ's steps, go where Christ has gone, and experience what Christ experienced. Murray emphasizes that this *can be done* when he says: "The mystery of the opened sanctuary is that we can enter, too. *The inner sanctuary, the Holiest of All, the presence of God, is the sphere of Christ's ministry and our life and service.*" [45]

Murray believes the author of Hebrews is revealing Christ's "chief glory" when he pronounces, "He is a Priest forever, a Priest in the power of an endless life, a Priest who opens to us the state of life into which He Himself has entered in, and a Priest who brings us there to live here on earth with the life of eternity in our bosom." [46]

Murray goes on to help the reader grasp the enormous significance of this profound revelation unfolded by the author of Hebrews: "Christian reader, do you know the power of this hope, entering into what is within the veil, where the Forerunner has already entered for us? *Jesus is in heaven for you, to secure you a life on earth in the power and joy of heaven*, to maintain the kingdom of heaven within you by that Spirit through whom God's will is done on earth as it is in heaven." [47]

Group Discussion

The Life Group began by expressing that this indelible hope is our spiritual eyes, and that Christ did the work of anchoring this hope in our souls firm and secure. Faith opens the heart in expectation, and in this hope God fulfills His promise. This is the work God does within us, as our souls enter the heavenly sanctuary with Christ and receive His blessings!

After this expression of hope, the group focused on enumerating those things which are free from God and some practical things for which the believer is responsible.

Based on Christ's atonement, the group indicated a few things as being among those which are free from God (i.e., they cannot be earned):

- Salvation
- Spiritual gifts
- Strength to fulfill His will

51

- Spiritual motivation
- Protection of one's soul
  (i.e., spiritual things that *only* God can do)

Based on Scripture, the group listed some items as being among the practical responsibility of the believer: (see lists in Lesson 3 & 4, as well)

- Engage in earnest prayer
- Abide by reading The Word
- Develop one's talents
- Be available to do God's will
- Put on the "full armor of God" to stand against temptation
- Work hard at employment to satisfy one's physical needs
- Live a disciplined life
  (i.e., physical things that the believer can to do)

The group returned to Murray's definition of Faith as a focus on those things which the believer is incapable of doing. Equally, the group was curious about the three ways in which Murray said hope might present itself: either as an "object of hope", or "what God does before us", or "the subjective grace [as a] disposition of hope in our hearts".

- The "object of hope" is clear; although, it requires Faith to grasp it.
- "What God does before us" is equally important, thus every *opportunity* that He puts before us should be taken very seriously. It could potentially be a very important leading from God that might take the believer in a critical direction where doing God's will leads to blessings for others. All legitimate *opportunities* that are without obvious temptations should be explored to the fullest for potential critical life-changing, faith-based action decisions.
- The "subjective grace [as a] disposition of hope in our heart" was seen as a reassuring, ever presence of the Holy Spirit that comforts the believer in knowing that God has not forgotten His promises during those long periods of diligence and perseverance.

The group felt that God puts into our hearts those desires He wants us to have, and, as such, His desires *can* become our desires, if we choose to accept them. God's purpose is to work "in" us all that He has promised, if we allow His desires to become our desires. The group returned to Murray's proclamation that our true inner selves can be found in the hope of our hearts; for it is there, in the depths of our desires, "where our hope lives".

The group completed the discussion by reiterating the importance of Jesus as High Priest. The believer can now follow Christ into His heavenly sanctuary each time he embraces Christ's ministry and a life in His service through the Holy Spirit.

There was consensus that believers can live this life on earth with an unquenching hope and joy of knowing with confidence and assurance that eternity awaits.

The kingdom of heaven is within each person who receives Christ's Spirit to dwell within, thus bringing God's kingdom on earth every time one emulates Christ in Faith, Hope, and Love.

Open My Eyes, That I May See [48]
Clara H. Scott (1841-1897)

Open my eyes, that I may see
Glimpses of truth Thou hast for me;
Place in my hand the wonderful key
That shall unclasp, and set me free.

Silently now I wait for Thee,
Ready, my God, Thy will to see
*Open my **eyes**, illumine me,*
Spirit divine!

Open my ears, that I may hear
Voices of truth Thou sendest clear;
And while the wave-notes fall on my ear,
Everything false will disappear.

Silently now I wait for Thee,
Ready, my God, Thy will to see
*Open my **ears**, illumine me,*
Spirit divine!

Open my mouth and let me bear
Gladly the warm truth everywhere
Open my heart and let me prepare
Love with Thy children thus to share.

Silently now I wait for Thee,
Ready, my God, Thy will to see
*Open my **heart**, illumine me,*
Spirit divine!

Open my mind, that I may read
More of Thy love in word and deed.
What shall I fear while Thou dost lead?
Only for light from Thee I plead.

Silently now I wait for Thee,
Ready, my God, Thy will to see
*Open my **mind**, illumine me,*
Spirit divine!

LESSON 6

Gifts & Dynamic Blessings
of The Promise

Life Group Meetings in March 2013
Scripture: see List of Scripture and Tables II & III

Presentation & Group Discussion

Having completed a very detailed reading, meditation, and discussion of each verse of Hebrews Chapter 6, the Life Group now turned its attention towards the gifts and blessings of The Promise. There are many promises throughout the Bible. Anyone interested in a comprehensive list of the promises should purchase a book, available from any Christian bookstore, that details these biblical promises. These books are often organized according to one's specific need. In this lesson, being focused on the epistle of Hebrews, one is dealing with either the free gifts of salvation through Jesus or the Inherited Blessings of the Holy Spirit, imparted by Jesus to believers after His resurrection.

Holly pointed out that there are many specific blessing in the Old Testament dealing with individual patriarchs and prophets (e.g., Abraham was promised he would be the father of many nations, etc.). Kimberley noted that there are many promises in Revelation dealing with the end-of-time. She listed seven such promises found in Revelation: 2:11, 2:17, 2:26-28, 3:5, and 3:21. In the former case, the promises of the Old Covenant to "God's chosen people" have been fulfilled. In the latter case, end-time promises will be realized at that time. These two areas are beyond the scope of this discussion. In this study, we are concerned with the divine dynamics of the present.

From the Bible's perspective the current time is that of the New Covenant, where Christ enables the Holy Spirit to dwell within those individuals who choose to know and obey His commandments (John 14:21). This indwelling of the Holy Spirit is the focus of this study, for the author of Hebrews is challenging those immature "born-again" Christians – who concentrate too much on the fundamentals of the Faith without necessarily applying them to their personal lives – to get beyond the mere relearning of the fundamentals. He encourages them to move on to *experiencing* Christ and the Holy Spirit within themselves through diligence, patience, perseverance, and endurance as a small part of Christ's suffering amidst their own personal experiences out in the real world of everyday life.

This lesson will deal with a look at some of the gifts and blessings of The Promise in two parts, as shown below in Tables II & III:

Table II   SALVATION – Fundamental Free Gifts of The Promise
Table III   SPIRITUAL GROWTH – Inherited Blessings of The Promise

These two tables do not necessarily represent comprehensive lists of these two areas, but they are some examples that were easy to find in Scripture. Again, if one desires a more complete list, the purchase of a book listing the promises of God is recommended.

SALVATION – Fundamental Free Gifts of The Promise

The New Testament is filled with "free gifts" of the New Covenant, which are available to anyone who desires salvation and eternal life. Although there are a few things one must do in their soul to accept these "free gifts", they cannot be earned, for *Christ earned them for ALL* through His atoning act of crucifixion and resurrection.

To accept these "free gifts" one generally needs do the following:

- Soften one's heart by a compassion for others
- Desire to know God
- Humble oneself and call upon Jesus for help
- Have a least the faith of a "mustard seed"
- Believe in their heart that Jesus was raised from the dead and verbally confess that belief before other people
- Turn one's life around and start living according to a biblical lifestyle (i.e., "repent of sins", etc.)
- Find a fellowship of believers and be baptized
- Ask God for help

This list of activities to humble oneself and to recognize the power of Jesus as the expected Messiah of the Jewish Old Covenant who would bring meaning and spiritual authority to this world, might seem like a lot to do; but, in fact, it can all be done in a matter of a few minutes. One need only remember the one criminal executed with Jesus who asked for His help (Luke 23:42-43). He showed compassion when he came to Jesus' defense, as the other criminal mocked Jesus for not physically "saving" Himself, as many thought He would do. The compassionate criminal chided his fellow ridiculing companion by saying they both deserved what they were getting, thus confessing his sinful behavior before Jesus and to those gathered around the cross. With what little faith he had, he asked Jesus to remember him when He came into His kingdom; thus acknowledging Jesus' authority and verbalizing his belief that Jesus would live, in some way, to help him beyond their crucifixions. Being symbolically baptized by the rain that fell upon them, Jesus imparted His grace by saying: "This very day you will be with me in paradise." The confession could not have been more simple. The humble criminal at Christ's side received the salvation of eternal life and the "free gifts" of The Promise.

Once received, the "free gifts" of salvation cannot be taken away or lost (see Romans Chapter 8), except by committing the "unpardonable" sin (Lesson 2). However, they can go unused or neglected, thus not becoming fully beneficial to the believer.

The Life Group reviewed a draft of Table II and revised it with additional Scripture.

Table II - SALVATION – Fundamental Free Gifts of The Promise

	What One Needs to Do	Free Gifts	Scripture
1	Soften heart (while a sinner)	God's Love, Christ's atonement	Rom. 5:8 Rom. 10:13
	Humble oneself enough to see one's need for Christ's love and to call upon Him for help		
	Desire to know God		
2	Have "mustard seed" of faith	Justification by God's grace	Rom. 3:23-24
3	Believe in heart Jesus was raised from dead and confess to others that Jesus is Lord	Salvation & Eternal Life	Rom. 10:9-10 Rom. 6:23
4	Repent, be baptized, and ask	Access to Holy Spirit (motivation)	Acts 2:38
•	Items 1-4 then automatic	Protection of Soul	Ps. 91:11 Ps. 121:7-8
•	Items 1-4 then automatic	Power, Love & Self-Control	II Tim. 1:7
•	Items 1-4 then automatic	Called Child of God	I John 3:1
•	Items 1-4 then ask God	Set Free from Bondage of Sin	Rom. 8:21
•	Items 1-4 then ask God	Wisdom	James 1:5
•	Items 1-4 then realize talents	Gifts of Spirit (individual talents)	Rom. 12:6-8

SPIRITUAL GROWTH – Inherited Blessings of The Promise

Being satisfied that Table II was a reasonably good list of the "free gifts" of The Promise, the Life Group turned its attention towards the Inherited Blessings of The Promise.

During Jesus' time, a servant master relationship was well understood. There was no "safety net" of social security, pensions, and the like; and every servant knew he was beholding to his master for survival. Servants were loyal and obedient to their masters, so they would be well treated in return. They held out some hope that when the master died they would receive something of an inheritance in exchange for many years of devoted service. The analogy is very clear: Jesus assured His followers who remained faithful servants until the end that they would inherit blessings of The Promise. These blessing differ from the "free gifts", however, in that one must be a patient enduring faithful servant. This means these blessings of The Promise are *conditioned* upon one's long term behavior. The Scriptures given below emphasize the point: (also see: I Thes. 2:9, II Tim 2:2-6, Pr. 14:23, 12:27, 18:9)

Hebrews 6:12

That *ye* be not *slothful*, but followers of them who through *faith* and *patience* inherit the promises. (KJV)

II Peter 1:5-6

Your goodness must be accompanied by knowledge, your knowledge by self-control, and your self-control by the *ability to endure*. [49]

James 5:11

Remember that it is those who have *patiently endured* to whom we accord the word *"blessed"*. [50]

I Timothy 4:8

Spiritual fitness [Godliness] is of unlimited value, for it holds promise both for the present life and the life to come. [51]

The Life Group turned its attention to II Timothy 2:1-6, where Paul is giving Timothy encouragement to endure with patience the hardships of his calling, as would a soldier on active duty, or an Olympic athlete in a contest, or a hard working farmer; who are all entitled to the rewards of their disciplined labor.

II Timothy 2:1-6

So, my son, be strong in the grace that Christ Jesus gives. Everything that you have heard me teach in public you should in turn entrust to reliable men, who will be able to pass it on to others. Put up with your share of hardship as a loyal soldier in Christ's army. Remember: 1. That no soldier on active service gets himself entangled in business, or he will not please his commanding officer. 2. A man who enters an athletic contest wins no prize unless he keeps the right rules laid down. 3. Only the man who works on the land has the right to the first share of its produce. Consider these three illustrations of mine and the Lord will help you to understand all that I mean. [52]

These three allegorical metaphors, which encompass human diligence, perseverance, patience, endurance, and hard work, speak volumes to the Promise Seeking believer who wishes to go beyond the fundamentals of Faith in search of Inherited Blessings of The Promise. Each of these human analogies requires that one be physically fit and suitably trained for the service of soldier, athlete, or farmer. They must know and understand the pursuit, and they must gain experience to achieve success. Also, it requires a certain higher level of fitness gained through repeated exercise and practice to attain a level of preparedness suitable to enter into full-time service of these professions. One may be a trained reservist, but that does not qualify him for the Special Forces; or one may be good at local sports, but that may not qualify him for a spot on an Olympic Team; or one may be an avid gardener, but that does not qualify him to be a full-time agronomist.

Each illustration draws attention to the need for one to be more fit physically and mentally for the service. For the Promise Seeking believer, the issue is being *spiritually fit* and courageous for the service to which God might call him in the everyday battle of good and evil. Scripture below sets the stage for this battle in the life of a Promise Seeking believer who chooses to engage in this *spiritual battle*, rather than remain in the training camp with the Salvation Satisfied believers, who prefer only to "lay over and over again" the fundamentals.

Ephesians 6:12

For our fight is not against any physical enemy: It is against organizations and powers that are *spiritual*. We are up against the unseen power that controls this dark world, and spiritual agents from the very headquarters of evil. [53]

For our struggle is not against flesh and blood, but against the rulers, against the powers, against the world forces of this darkness, against *spiritual forces* of wickedness in the heavenly places. (NASB)

II Corinthians 10:3-4

The truth is that, although we lead normal human lives, the battle we are fighting is on the *spiritual level.* The very weapons we use are not human but powerful in God's warfare for the destruction of the enemy's strongholds. [54]

For though we walk in the flesh, we do not war according to the flesh, for the weapons of our warfare are not of the flesh, but divinely powerful for the destruction of the fortresses. (NASB)

II Timothy 1:7

For God has not given us a spirit of cowardice, but a spirit of power and love and a sound mind. [55]

For God has not given us a spirit of timidity, but of power and love and discipline. (NASB)

These passages strongly indicate that the spiritual growth of the Promise Seeking believer is for the purpose of developing Spiritual Fitness and for boldly using the power of love and a sound mind to practice sacrificial love on the real spiritual "battlefield" of life.

To focus on the second allegory, I told Ellen, who loves to ski, that I had a (hypothetical) "free gift" for her. It was a gift that thousands of people would love to have at almost any cost. Many work extremely hard for the item, but never have enough to attain it. The gift is from the U.S. Olympic Committee, and the gift is a position on the United States Winter Olympic ski team. She does not need to go to any trials, and she does not need to earn the position on the team; it is a free gift. So, now that she has the gift: what is she going to do with it? Well, its obvious that if she is going to represent the United States with honor, she will need to practice. She will need to be physically and mentally prepared to compete in the events. Although the position on this team may be free, there are very serious responsibilities, which are necessary in order to use the gift to honor those who gave it to her.

The same analogy can be applied to the Promise Seeking Christian. God's free gift of grace is like being chosen for the universal spiritual Olympic team, without having done anything to earn the right to be on it. Christ, through the Holy Spirit, will give the Promise Seeking believer the spiritual power of Faith, Hope, and Love; but it is up to the believer to develop the Spiritual Fitness appropriate for the contest to which they will be entered. How many people have received this free gift of spiritual grace, yet never study the rules, never practice the Faith, and, in fact, rarely ever show up for the event; or if they do, find themselves very unprepared to engage in the sacrificial love of disciplined "longsuffering" necessary to win the day.

In the Heart – Not on the Cuff

It is important to understand that the author of Hebrews was trying to get these Salvation Satisfied Christians out of their comfortable surroundings of the religious community, and to go beyond the fundamentals of the Faith, to experiencing the Holy Spirit by their ACTIONS outside the Christian camp into a secular world, where human encounters happen. To express one's belief verbally among fellow believers is one thing; but going out among unbelievers and acting out the kindness, generosity, and benevolence of sacrificial love is altogether another matter, for one is going to be used and abused. This, however, is exactly what Christ calls upon His followers to do. Go out into the world and demonstrate this *agape* love and patiently endure the consequences. It means that the Promise Seeking believer must truly "wear" the Holy Spirit in their heart and not "on their cuff", so to speak.

Although the combat casualties of this spiritual conflict are very visible, the war for souls itself is largely invisible. As such, one is not necessarily talking about just going to church, although that can be helpful in learning the Gospel and worshiping; or participating in a community religious program, although those may be of value in building fellowship with other believers; or engaging in some emotional ritual, even though that may have some significance in enriching one's personal commitment to a religious preference. *No, spiritual battles are, for the most part, fought in private.* One must take Jesus' words, recorded in Matthew Chapter 6, to heart, at face value, and quite seriously.

Matthew 6:1-6

> "Beware of doing your good deeds conspicuously to catch men's eyes or you will miss the reward of your Heavenly Father. So, when you do good to other people, don't hire a trumpeter to go in front of you – like those play-actors in the synagogues, and streets who make sure that men admire them. Believe me, they have had all the reward they are going to get! No, when you give to charity, don't let your left hand know what your right hand is doing, so that your giving may be secret. *Your Father who knows all secrets will reward you.* And then, when you pray, don't be like the play-actors. They love to stand and pray in the synagogues and at street-corners so that people may see them at it. Believe me, they have all the reward they are going to get. But when you pray, go into your own room, shut the door and pray to your Father privately. *Your Father who sees all private things will reward you.*" [56]

The domain of the mature, spiritually fit Promise Seeking servant of Christ is to know Christ's commandments and to obey them (John 14:21); in order to develop one's Spiritual Fitness privately, so one can emulate Christ-like sacrificial love in one's behavior without fanfare. It is said, "Actions speak louder than words." Here Jesus is instructing the Promise Seeking servant to do one's "good deeds" inconspicuously, in private or secret, so as to not draw attention to oneself. It may be sufficient – and probably inconsequential – for only the one to whom the good deed is rendered to know the act, and in many cases even the recipient need not know the identity of the benefactor. Jesus further emphasized the importance of doing things in secret, when He said in Matthew 6:16-18.

Matthew 6:16-18

"Then, when you fast, don't look like those miserable play-actors. For they deliberately disfigure their faces so that people may see that they are fasting. Believe me, they have had all their reward. No, when you fast, anoint your head and wash your face so that nobody knows that you are fasting – let it be a secret between you and your Father. And your Father who knows all secrets will reward you." [57]

Jesus gave these instructions to do good deeds, to pray, and to fast in secret; so that the desires of one's heart would be genuinely motivated, and that his rewards in heaven would be great. Further, He advised more completely that one's entire life should be so aligned as to stay focused on heaven rather than on earth, when He said:

Matthew 6:19-21

"Don't pile up treasures on earth, where moth and rust can spoil them and thieves can break in and steal. But keep your treasure in Heaven where there is neither moth nor rust to spoil it and nobody can break in and steal. For wherever your treasure is, your heart will be there too!" [58]

Often one sees a very prosperous individual, who may live in the finest home, drive the newest vehicles, own the nicest furniture, take the most exotic vacations, sport the most envious activities, rise to the most prominent positions, and receive the greatest accolades for community service; to which one may hear the phrase: "Isn't that person blessed?" Well, the answer is – a resounding NO!!! His prosperity may be abundant, due to his own efforts, but his Inherited Blessings may be few. The outward appearance of one's position in the world (i.e., his treasures on earth) is no indication and no measure of Inherited Blessings (i.e., treasures in heaven) from God to a mature Promise Seeking believer. One cannot, and should not, judge such an individual from afar, as they may have some spiritual blessing or none at all. Only by getting to know such an individual personally can an assessment be made, and even then it should not be voiced.

I gave an example to the group of once having met a woman, named Lois, who was a longtime friend of Marilyn's family. We visited her only once for several hours while travelling, just to say hello. She lived on a back lot and seemed to own very little. I only remember that in this short visit she radiated with Faith, Hope, and Love. Irrespective of her rather limited circumstances, her attitude towards life was one of the most positive I had ever encountered. Just being in her presence seemed to lift one's spirits. She was truly blessed with a Godly spirit; even though she had few possessions, and she had endured many hardships.

Another example I gave was that of an assistant director of a community college, where I once taught for three years before returning to graduate school to get a Ph.D.. This gentleman had been a missionary in China for ten years before returning to the United States. In addition to his day job at the college, he was a full-time minister of a local church, and, on the side, he bought houses, fixed them up, and then rented them at little or no profit to the underprivileged. I got to know this individual quite well, as we had lunch together frequently. We socialized outside work, where I observed that he and his family lived quite modestly, in spite of his resources. I still think of him as one of the most mature Christians it has been my privilege to know. On one occasion, I asked him what he thought he could do to mature more in his Faith, as "growing in Christ" was the topic of the lunch conversation. He hesitated, took a moment to contemplate, then said he would like to be prepared (i.e., spiritually fit) enough to handle absolutely any situation or circumstance God would lead him into, or be so directed by the Holy Spirit to pursue. For many Christians that is a tall order, but it was the same goal as that of the Apostle Paul. It should be the goal of every maturing Promise Seeking servant of Christ.

By going through the Bible and extracting some of the *conditional* Inherited Blessings of The Promise, one can generate Table III. This list was constructed as they came to mind. The first column lists an Inherited Blessing; the second column lists the *conditional* Spiritual Fitness necessary for the Promise Seeking servant to realize some degree of blessing; and the third column is the Scripture backing up the condition. The Life Group went over the list of Inherited Blessings and made a few revisions and corrections.

The group discussed what was necessary for the Promise Seeking believer to do to inherit these blessings. It is like saying: if one had a thoroughbred race horse who had a blood line from a famous horse like Man-O-War, but the young horse never had a trainer, and never exercised, and never practiced, and never ran a race; then he would certainly not "*inherit*" and demonstrate the abilities of his ancestor. In like manner, the

Promise Seeking believer must train, exercise, practice, and run the race, to emulate the character of Christ, his forerunner, and to inherit these greater blessings on earth and rewards in heaven. Is this not a worthy ambition for one's life?

Someone recited Romans 8:28 from memory: "In all things, God works for the good of those who love him and are called according to His purpose." J. B. Phillips translates this passage from the ancient Greek: "Moreover we know that to those who *love* God, who are *called* according to his plan, everything that happens fits into a pattern for good." So, one must *love* God and pursue one's *calling*, then and only then will those things which "happen" work into a "pattern for good" – like George Bailey in "It's a Wonderful Life". It may be for your good in heaven, but another person's good on earth. One should not be confused as to how God "works" out "a pattern for good" amongst those who *actively* love Him by fulfilling Jesus' commandments.

In looking over this short list of *conditional* Inherited Blessings of The Promise, one can see some rewards in heaven, some state-of-being in general, but most of all, one can see that many of these Inherited Blessings are the *spiritual tools*, the heavenly equipment, and the divine skills to fight the spiritual battles; in order to win the spiritual contests and to cultivate spiritual growth here on earth.

Reiterating what the Apostle Paul said to Timothy: "*Spiritual Fitness* is of unlimited value, for it holds promise both for the present life and the life to come" (I Tim. 4:8, Phillips). This is the goal of the Promise Seeking servant of Christ: to become *Spiritually Fit* by diligent perseverant striving through "longsuffering" to acquire these Inherited Blessings of The Promise, in order to fight the good fight, to win the contest, and to harvest the souls for eternal life, by exhibiting genuine sacrificial Christ-like loving character in this dark world.

Table III - SPIRITUAL GROWTH – Inherited Blessings of The Promise

Inherited Blessing	Spiritual Fitness of a Seeking Servant	Scripture
Abundant, Spirit-filled Life	"ask" in prayer, "seek" in Word, and "knock" on doors in real life for God-given opportunities	Matt. 7:7 John 10:10
Peace Beyond Understanding	in everything with prayer and thanksgiving	Phil. 4:6-7
Renewed Strength	wait on the Lord in "longsuffering" wait with diligence and perseverance	Is. 40:31 Rom. 8:25
Joyful Shouting	tears of affliction from earnest evangelists	Ps. 126:5-6
Hope Eternal	make deepest desires of one's heart God's desires to anchor soul in Christ, our Heavenly High Priest	Heb. 6:19

Full love of God & Christ; indwelling comfort & guide of Holy Spirit; things work together in pattern of good	(i) know & obey Christ's three commandments (ii) listen with "polished ear" to Holy Spirit (iii) act on one's "calling" & do God's will	John 14:21 John 14:26 Rom. 8:28
Forgiveness of Transgressions	forgive others	Mat. 6:14-15
Heirs to Kingdom of Heaven	(i) know one's need for God (ii) suffer persecution for Christ's sake	Mat. 5:3 Mat. 5:10
Comfort & Encouragement	know what it means to be sorrowful suffer to encourage others in their suffering	Mat. 5:4 II Cor. 1:5
Salt of Earth	be humble, stake-a-claim to nothing, and witness	Mat. 5:5
Satisfied Inner Spirit	hunger and thirst for true righteousness	Mat. 5:6
Mercy from God	show mercy to others	Mat. 5:7
Ability to See God	be utterly sincere & wholeheartedly genuine	Mat. 5:8
Called Sons of God	make peace with everyone	Mat. 5:9
Great Reward in Heaven	let yourself be persecuted, slandered, insulted for Christ's sake	Mat. 5:11
Never go Hungry or Be in Need	work at a job to the best of one's abilities	II Thes.3:10
Heavenly Reward for Work	work at a job cheerfully, as if for the Lord and not to impress your employer	Eph. 6:7-8 Col. 3:23-24
Boundless Power of Spiritual Strength against Evil	put on full armor of God: integrity, truth, gospel of peace, salvation, Holy Spirit, Word of God, Faith, and pray at all times with all kinds of prayer, keep alert, and persist in effectual fervent prayer	Eph. 6:10-18
Happiness in Hope	endure trials patiently with a habit of prayer	Rom. 12:12
Fullness of Christ	attain maturity by development of gifts	Eph. 4:11-13
Ask in Prayer and God shall Hear the Righteous and it shall be Done on Earth or in Heaven According to His will	(i) abide in Christ and let Christ abide in you (ii) continually do God's will to abide fully (iii) pray according to God's will (iv) pray fervently & be righteous	John 15:7 I John 2:17 I John 5:14 James 5:16
Christ-Like Character	in one's life plant, grow, prune, & cultivate (by crucifying one's flesh, passions, & desires) the "tree of life" in order to show forth fruits of the Spirit: love, joy, peace, patience, kindness, generosity, fidelity, tolerance, and self-control	Gal 5:22-25

Jesus' Call to Spiritual Fitness

Life Group Meeting in early April 2013
Scripture: see List of Scripture

Maturing into Spiritual Adulthood

The author of Hebrews is challenging these Jewish Christians to grow-up in their Faith by becoming Spiritually Fit, mature believers; who are mentally equipped, conditionally exercised, and selflessly disciplined for the spiritual struggle between the powers of this world and the next. Repeating what Paul said to the Corinthians:

I Corinthians 14:20

> Don't be children but use your intelligence! By all means be innocent as babes as far as evil is concerned, but where your minds are concerned be full grown men! [59]

Further, Paul implored the Corinthians to wake-up, own-up, and grow-up; for the day was coming when they would stand before God without pretense. Paul took them by the shoulders and shook them into solemn reflection by saying:

I Corinthians 13:11-12

> When I was a little child I talked and felt and thought like a child. Now that I am a man, I have finished with childish things. At present we are men looking at puzzling reflections in a mirror. The time will come when we shall see reality whole and face to face! At present all I know is a little fraction of the truth, but the time will come when I shall know it as fully as God has known me! [60]

Returning to Paul's three allegories of a soldier fighting, an athlete competing, and a farmer cultivating, he presents to Timothy the need to concentrate on Spiritual Fitness (I Timothy 4:7-8). One can surmise the consequences of being unprepared by posing the following questions with Scripture references.

Might one someday find himself on a *spiritual battlefield* and discover he is without adequate defenses to "stand firm" and resist evil, or too inexperienced in the use of the "sword of the Spirit" to come out victorious? What if he finds himself without enough genuine righteousness to invoke a credible integrity, or without a sufficient grasp of the truth, or not having walked enough in the gospel of peace, or without a firm knowledge of salvation, or without sufficient understanding of the Word of God, or without a solid shield of Faith? These are elements of Spiritual Fitness referred to as the "full armor of God" in Ephesians 6:10-18.

Or might one someday find himself presented with an *Olympic spiritual contest* of defending the Faith by an example of Christ-like Love, and discover one's behavior too easily loses patience, or does not look for ways to be constructive, or is too anxious to impress, or is cherishing inflated ideas of one's own importance, or is not well mannered, or is pursuing selfish advantage, or is being too touchy and on edge, or is taking account of others wrong doing, or is gloating over the wickedness of others, or is not being joyous with those who know the truth, or is not enduring difficult circumstances, or is giving up on trust, or is failing to have hope, or is just not committing oneself to the care for those closest to him? These elements of Spiritual Fitness all refer to Jesus' definition of Love in I Corinthians 13:3-7.

Or might one someday find himself called upon *to plant seeds of Faith, or to cultivate a field of lost souls,* and find that the life-giving fruits of the Spirit are without sufficient produce of love, joy, peace, patience, kindness, generosity, fidelity, tolerance, or self-control to emulate a Christ-like character adequate enough for these lost souls to truly see the light of life within the believer's being? These elements of Spiritual Fitness are the "fruits of the Spirit", found in Galatians 5:22-25.

One should reflect solemnly on his current spiritual state and ask: Have I conquered those habits of spiritual childhood that hold one in immaturity or in a state which lacks seriousness? One needs to listen closely to Paul's words to the Ephesians when he said:

Ephesians 5:4

> The key-note of your conversation should not be coarseness or silliness or flippancy – which are quite out of place, but *a sense of all that we owe to God.* [61]

Some day we will stand before God without any of the "treasures" of this world to clothe us, but only with the righteousness of our "treasures" in heaven. How naked might we be, if we do not in this world earnestly strive to be Spiritually Fit?

A Volunteer Service for Spiritual Warfare – A Private Army

Returning to what is said in Matthew Chapter 6 regarding doing one's good deeds, fasting, and praying in secret, Jesus calls upon His spiritual special services to do most of their work in private. This is so they will remain humble and not miss out on their reward in heaven. Equally, Jesus calls for volunteers. No one is conscripted into this private army to engage in spiritual warfare by extending sacrificial love to those who may largely abuse him, or who may not appreciate the effort, or who may insult, cheat, slander, and persecute him, or even kill him in some circumstances. No, this is a purely volunteer army, for the fight to save souls is very personal. Recall what the author of Hebrews said to these Jewish Christians:

Hebrews 6:1-3

> Let us leave behind the elementary teaching *about* Christ and go forward to *adult understanding.* Let us not lay over and over again the foundational truths: repentance from the deeds which led to death, believing in God, the teaching of baptism, laying-on of hands, belief in the resurrection of the dead, and the final judgment. *No, if God allows, let us go on.* [62]

Given the very voluntary, personal, and private nature of this spiritual warfare, one cannot and should not fault any of the Salvation Satisfied Christians who choose to remain behind in the fellowship of brotherly believers. Remember, they may have their reward already, so let them enjoy it. Salvation is free, and these Salvation Satisfied believers will be in heaven; whether or not they took the author of Hebrews' advice and moved on to a Promise Seeking life with the Holy Spirit. God is overjoyed that any confessing brethren is no longer lost.

For others, however, "*if God allows, let us go on*", and get beyond just repeating foundational truths, but *experience* a life alive in the Holy Spirit released by APPLICATION of one's Faith; thus becoming full heirs of The Promise. If one takes Scripture at face value, and there is no reason why one should not, the "rewards" of the Promise Seeking believer, who lives by "obedience to the promptings of the Spirit" (Rom. 8:4), will inherit blessings far greater than one can imagine. In this life, one cannot fully ascertain the magnitude of these blessings; however, the one who trusts in Faith, Hope, and Love, can experience a "foretaste of the Spirit" (Rom. 8:23), which cannot be taken away (Rom. 8:38-39).

Spiritual Maturity Begins with the Holy Spirit

Spiritual maturity BEGINS with the Holy Spirit! Every "born-again" believer has access to the Holy Spirit, but full expression of the Spirit is NOT automatic; for one must ACT

ON FAITH for the Holy Spirit to express Himself. One is overjoyed to see the emotional enthusiasm of a new believer who is experiencing the power of the Holy Spirit for the first time and becoming involved in all sorts of activities. This, however, is *not* the spiritual maturity or *Spiritual Fitness* of which the author of Hebrews speaks. Such maturity in Christ and Spiritual Fitness comes by APPLYING the power of the Holy Spirit to one's everyday behavior over a long period of time by diligence, perseverance, patient endurance, and "longsuffering".

One can guess that many a seminary graduate has ventured onto the spiritual battlefield thinking his brief education was sufficient for the task; only to discover that the battle first requires some long term maturing in *Spiritual Fitness*. Only then has the Promise Seeking believer become equipped for the "special services combat" on the spiritual battlefield.

Paul speaks of this BEGINNING by the Spirit being *within* oneself when he writes to the Romans:

Romans 8:9-11

> You are not carnal but spiritual, if the Spirit of God finds a home within you. You cannot, indeed, be a Christian at all unless you have something of his Spirit in you. Now if Christ does live within you his presence means that your sinful nature is dead, but your spirit becomes alive because of the righteousness he brings with him. Once the Spirit of him who raised Christ Jesus from the dead lives within you, he will, by that same Spirit, bring to your whole being, yes even your mortal bodies, a new strength and vitality. For he now lives in you. [63]

The Spirit is now within one's being. The soul is no longer empty. The living water of life is now within the human vessel, the Holy Temple of the body (I Corinthians 6:19). However, the living water of the Holy Spirit does NOT come out of the vessel by itself, on its own; any more than the water behind a dam pours forth without someone raising the gates. It is the RESPONSIBILITY of the Promise Seeking believer to access the Holy Spirit through Faith by ACTING on the *conditional* statements of Scripture, mostly provided by Jesus himself, (see Table III, Lesson 6) to inherit blessings of The Promise; that will, in turn, CONDITION him to become MORE easily responsive to the higher nature of the Spirit, rather than to the lower nature of human instincts. With each iteration of this progressive growth, the Promise Seeking believer becomes more Spiritually Fit and more equipped to go out on the spiritual battlefield. In essence, it is the APPLICATION OF THE SPIRIT IN PRACTICE TO ONE'S OWN BEHAVIOR in every minute of every day, steadily through diligence, perseverance, and patient endurance of "longsuffering" that builds the *Spiritual Fitness*, by releasing the Holy Spirit and continually inheriting more blessings of The Promise (see Table III, Lesson 6).

Going back to Lesson 3, one can see below the progressive developmental stages of experiencing Christ and sharing in His suffering. These stages are an integral part of maturing in *Spiritual Fitness*.

To *experience* Christ and *share* in his suffering one must:

stage I   be filled with the Holy Spirit,

stage II   trust God fully,

stage III   surrender one's self-will fully to God's will,

stage IV   genuinely live a moral life with utmost honesty in all things,

stage V   care about others more than self in every situation,

stage VI   abide through prayer and forgiveness always, and

stage VII   step-out in personal acts of Faith that might lead to "longsuffering".

Being filled with the Holy Spirit is the FIRST stage in spiritual development. After that comes trust, surrender, living a moral life, caring for others, abiding in prayer, and stepping out in acts of Faith. All of these stages are things a Promise Seeking believer does in PRACTICE by the power of the Holy Spirit to develop Spiritual Fitness. It is a REPETITIVE progression (or iterative cycle); whereby, one gets better with PRACTICE (or improves with each cycle). This means of growth can be compared and contrasted against those things an athlete might do in practice to develop physical fitness for competition in a sport. This returns us to Paul's allegory regarding an athlete developing his physical condition to compete in the Olympic games to that of a Promise Seeking believer developing his spiritual condition to run the "good race" of life.

Spiritual "Discipline" and "Exercise" are Necessary for Godliness

Table IV compares the means of growth in physical fitness to that of Spiritual Fitness. Utilizing the precepts outlined in this table, a Promise Seeking believer builds Spiritual Fitness as the message of Jesus Christ is put into practice, little by little, over a long period of time, in the same manner as one might develop one's physical fitness skills in a sport. (see Table IV)

Parents can remember when a young child first took to the soccer field. The children with great enthusiasm followed a ball around the field like a small herd of puppies chasing the ball in random directions. Then, as years passed, they grew and became more knowledgeable, skilled, and proficient. Then the day came, while in middle school, when their son saved the game with a diving block. Then came the day during a tournament, when their son, almost finished with high school and perhaps one of the best goalies in the league, guarded the net with precision by dynamically moving from side to side, staying alert for any action of the opposing team, and keeping his eyes sharply focused on the ball. The same is true with Spiritual Fitness, as Paul explained to the Corinthians in Chapter 13. When he was a child he talked, felt, and thought like a child, but when he grew-up, he put away childish things and behaved as a disciplined adult with a sound mind.

True Spiritual Fitness grows over time the same way a child grows in the development of skills in a sport. One is truly "born-again" when the believer begins to *actually keep* Jesus' commandments; allowing God to make His home within his being and to enable the Holy Spirit to come alive (John 14:21). At that moment the Holy Spirit is awakened within the believer. He begins reading the Word of God seriously for the first time with the aid of the Holy Spirit as his guide. Understanding some of Jesus' spiritual message, he denies a little of himself and finds himself praying for someone in need. Listening to the "promptings" of the Holy Spirit, he gets an idea of how to help that person. Without any grandstanding, he *acts on Faith* to show some true righteousness to that individual. As a result of this act, some consequences may unfold that lead him into undeserved suffering. Once having patiently endured the Christ-like suffering as a servant and waiting on God, he discovers, one day, he has inherited a blessing (see Table III, Lesson 6). Circumstances seem to be working together like they never have before, and more opportunities are presenting themselves to him to repeat this means of growth. As he repeats the cycle over and over again, each successive opportunity leads him to grow, rise, and prosper in Spiritual Fitness to where God leads him to do things he never thought imaginable. His life changes completely as he meets new people, moves on to new opportunities, and grows confident in every aspect of life. Although he remains humble and practices his "righteousness" in private, the "good works" of his heart, honed by this progressive growth in Spiritual Fitness, have built an integrity that, unbeknownst to him, shines a refreshing new invigorating life; radiantly illuminating Spirit into the lifeless world around him, like a bright light placed upon a stand.

One increases in Spiritual Fitness by *repeating* this means of abiding and doing God's will over an over again, thus mounting up Inherited Blessings:

hear the Word of Christ → **deny** self → **pray** in ALL things → **listen** to Holy Spirit → **act** on Faith → **care** for others → **suffer** as Christ → **wait** on God → **inherit** blessings (Item 5, Table IV).

In exercising this Spiritual Fitness iteration cycle, one needs to read Matthew Chapter 5 in its entirety and grasp its whole meaning. This chapter is about building one's inner Spiritual Fitness to go beyond the Law. Jesus speaks of how even "the smallest letter or stroke" of the Jewish Law (Matt. 5:18) and the prophecies of the Old Covenant will be fulfilled with His own death and resurrection by bringing the Holy Spirit to live within each believer. The Law will be fulfilled in Spirit by actually *going beyond it*. Paul clarified this in Romans Chapter 8. He writes:

Romans 8:1-4

> "There is therefore now no condemnation for those who are in Christ Jesus. For the law of the Spirit of life in Christ Jesus has set you free from the law of sin and of death. For what the Law could not do, weak as it was through the flesh, God *did*: sending His *own* Son in the likeness of sinful flesh and *as an offering* for sin, He condemned sin in the flesh, in order that the requirement of the Law might be fulfilled in us, who do not walk according to the flesh, but according to the Spirit." (NASB)

After giving the beatitudes, Jesus repeats some of the Law; then indicates how one will be able to *go beyond it* by the power of the Holy Spirit. The Law said one shall not murder, but Jesus said you shall not even be angry with your brother; the Law said one shall not commit adultery, but Jesus said you shall not even lust after anyone; the Law said one shall not lie, but Jesus said you shall be so impeccably honest that you will have no need for oaths, for you will need only say "yes" or "no" to any accusation; the Law said one had the right to recompense for any infraction, but Jesus said let evil have its way with you, let yourself be wronged, and if someone asks something of you, give him more than he asks; the Law said one should love his neighbor, but Jesus said you shall be able to even love your enemy, for what credit is it to love a friend, even non-believers do that; no, you shall even love those who hate you and persecute you; for you shall be able, by the power of the Holy Spirit, to be wholeheartedly genuine and morally "perfect as your heavenly Father is perfect" (Matthew 5:21-48). Never forget, however, that you are only *striving at your utmost* to give thanks to God by returning His Love to people around you, for Jesus said:

Matthew 19:17

> "There is only One who is good; but if you wish to enter into life, keep the commandments." (NASB)

Table IV - Physical Fitness vs. Spiritual Fitness

	Physical Fitness in Sports	Spiritual Fitness of a Promise Seeking Believer
1	- good bodily health for performance	- your body is the Temple of the Holy Spirit; it needs "living water" and "solid food" from The Word (I Corinthians 6:19)
2	- what goes into body effects strength	- what your eye desires is what fills the soul; either human nature or "light of life" dominates, not both (Matthew 6:22-24; Luke 11:34)
3	- start sport skills practice at an early age to ensure they become second-nature with growth	- when "born-again" and filled with the Holy Spirit, develop early spiritual skills of kindness, generosity, and self-control until they become second-nature
4	- learn the rules of the sport and follow them avidly and in detail (or your win may be disqualified)	- learn an "adult understanding" of the Word of God, so as not to be deceived; know what Jesus' commanded and follow them honestly (John 14:21) (Table III, Lesson 6)
5	- exercise, practice, compete = good - exercise, practice, compete = better - exercise, practice, compete = best	- in ALL allow the Holy Spirit to grow character: - **hear** Word of Christ, **deny** self, **pray** in ALL things, **listen** to the Holy Spirit, **act** on Faith, **care** for others, **suffer** as Christ, **wait** on God, **inherit** blessing. Repeat this iteration in practice, over and over again
6	- be a part of sports teams anywhere and participate in the game	- become a part of fellowships wherever you live and do not just sit on the bench
7	- develop mental discipline; avoid bad speech habits; be a "good sport"	- develop self-control over speech; eliminate character traits that destroy integrity: "but what proceeds out of the mouth, this defiles the man." (Matthew 15:11)
8	- improvement comes after many years of hard work, injuries, defeats, discouragements, etc.	- inheriting spiritual blessings of Godliness come after years of diligence, perseverance, and endurance of "doing what is right" in God's sight
9	- get to know those good in the sport; practice with them; and observe professionals engaged in the sport	- learn from behavior of mature believers; engage in activities with Holy Spirit filled people; and seek out guidance from God's ordained

10	- move to higher levels in the sport by challenging oneself to learn more complicated athletic skills	- take more seriously *conditional* activities of spiritual growth from Scripture and search for more inherited blessings of The Promise (Table III, Lesson 6)
11	- excel to the highest competition level available at one's skill set	- strive for a deep and wholeheartedly genuine Holy Spirit filled character from one's Spiritual Fitness
12	- experience the heartache of as many competitions as possible over a long time to become an expert in the sport	- experience the consequences of doing God's will and enduring patiently the *"longsuffering"* of trials; whereby, one's Faith is annealed by fire

Unconscious Integrity Reflects the Inward "Good Works" of Spiritual Fitness

Immediately after Matthew Chapter 5 comes Matthew 6:1, where Jesus directs believers to do their "righteousness" in private, so as not to lose the rewards of Inherited Blessings. This is not a contradiction to doing "good works" so all can see, as Jesus ordered in Matthew 5:16. These "good works" are what the Holy Spirit is doing in the believer to build up a Christ-like character through Spiritual Fitness. It is the well developed, *Spiritually Fit Christ-like character* that the world will see; not all the internal "good works" of preparation, exercise, and practice that went on behind the scenes. No, it is the RESULT of those "good works" done on one's heart that will be *unconsciously* reflected in one's integrity, not the many secret deeds of genuine "righteousness" done along the way in building up the Spiritual Fitness by release of the Holy Spirit's power.

To illustrate this point, here is a true story. There was a man who worked at a company for many years. There was another employee at the same company, who, on infrequent occasions, would run into this man, and they would have a brief conversation. Their paths had crossed once before in another organization, but they had not developed a close friendship, only a professional relationship. When the man retired, the acquaintance came to this man's retirement dinner to say good-bye. To the man's surprise, the admirer said, "I am glad we knew each other, for you changed my life." After the dinner, the man thought to himself; how could I have possibly changed this man's life, I barely knew him; we interacted in our line of work and we spoke in passing, but we never talked about anything of a personal nature. The truth is, one does not know how much one's example impacts the lives of those who are watching.

Releasing the Holy Spirit Requires Real Practice

The living water of Life is in its Holy Vessel, like the water behind a dam, but one must open the gates. Does one send a child to open the gates of a large dam? No, he probably could not ever budge the large wheel. One might, however, direct the child to a small dammed-up stream where the wheel is smaller and provide him some assistance. The same is true with growing in Spiritual Fitness by releasing the power of the Holy Spirit. One can follow the mechanisms given in Table IV (particularly Item 5) and practice small acts of kindness and generosity to build up at least some level of Spiritual Fitness; then once fit, one might attempt turning the next larger wheel on the gate of righteousness.

One cannot develop this Spiritual Fitness by just participating in the social programs of a religious organization. The meaning of Hebrews 6:1-3 is clear: if one goes to church each Sunday and talks about repentance, reaffirms belief in God, teaches baptism, lays on hands, expresses belief in the resurrection, and proclaims the final judgment – *they remain just a Salvation Satisfied believer*; no matter how many times they "lay over and over again" these truths week after week and year after year. "No, if God allows, let us go on" to learning how to release the power of the Holy Spirit in PRACTICE and build *Spiritual Fitness*, so we may enjoy the Inherited Blessings of The Promise.

The goal of the Promise Seeking believer is to understand in depth the cause and effect relationship between the *conditional* statements of Scripture, (Table III, Lesson 6) and to discipline oneself to PRACTICE AND APPLY these concepts to the utmost of one's ability. Remember what Paul said to Timothy:

I Timothy 4:7-8 (underlined words for text comparison)

> Take time and trouble to keep yourself spiritually fit. Bodily fitness has a limited value, but Spiritual fitness is of unlimited value, for it holds promise both for the present life and the life to come. [64]

> Discipline yourself for the purpose of godliness; for bodily discipline is only of little profit but godliness is profitable for all things, since it holds promise for the present life and for the life to come. (NASB)

> Exercise thyself rather unto godliness. For bodily exercise profiteth little, but godliness is profitable unto all things, having promise of the life that now is and of that which is to come. (KJV)

Spiritual Fitness increases as one understands the *conditional* statements in Scripture and fulfills them by the power of the Holy Spirit, through "discipline", "exercise", and taking "time and trouble" to be Holy. This is not always easy to do, for the selfish desires of one's heart (i.e., human nature) are diametrically opposed to the heart of God, a Christ-like character, and the Holy Spirit. One must deny self and direct one's attention towards the sacrificial care of others. It is totally against human instinct for one to surrender one's own desires and to give over their efforts in care of others. However, this is exactly what Jesus asks people to do in His three direct commandments:

- Care about and serve God with all your heart, mind, soul, and strength [65]
- Care for your neighbor (anyone in the world) as you would yourself [66]
- Care for "one another" (disciples) to the point of sacrificing your life [67]

Jesus gave the first two of these commandments as being the most important of God's commandments, as He said, "The whole of the Law and the Prophets depends on these two commandments." (Matt. 22:40)

The old Jewish Law (Mitzvot) is composed of 613 individual strict rules for living (365 one should not do and 248 one should do). [68] One *cannot earn Salvation* nor achieve righteousness by following the rules of the old Jewish Law; however good intentioned one might be, for it is impossible for anyone to keep all the Law. Paul said, "The Law never succeeded in producing righteousness – the failure was always the weakness of human nature" (Rom. 8:3), but God was able to provide a way of enabling righteousness to come to earth through the Holy Spirit, by offering His son as a sacrifice for our "iniquity". So, with Christ's crucifixion, resurrection, and atoning salvation by grace, a believer – "born-again" in the Spirit – is no longer bound by the Jewish Old Covenant Law. Instead, being free of the Law, he is *voluntarily* called by Jesus to follow the Spirit of the Law, by being obedient to the "promptings" of the Holy Spirit.

This means that Jesus came to fulfill the Law by enabling the *Spirit of the Law* to live within each believer. He encouraged those unfamiliar with His Spirit message to grasp a full understanding of how with the *Spirit one could go beyond the Law.* When asked by the young rich ruler, what point of the Law he needed to do to be "good" and obtain eternal life, Jesus said no one was good but God; but if he wanted to try to be "good" he should at least follow the basic commandments:

Matthew 19:18-19

> And Jesus said, "You shall not commit murder; you shall not commit adultery; you shall not steal; you shall not bear false witness; honor your father and mother; and you shall love your neighbor as yourself." (NASB)

The rich young ruler said he had done each of these, and asked Jesus what else he needed to do to receive eternal life. To this Jesus said he needed to sell all he owned and give the proceeds to the poor, then follow Him; for Jesus knew he worshiped his property. Because of the "weakness of human nature", the man could not give up his possessions and follow Jesus, so he went away. From this experience, Jesus told his disciples that it was impossible for men to do anything on their own to obtain eternal life, but "with God all things are possible" (Matt. 19:26). By His death and resurrection, they later saw how salvation could be obtained by the free-gift of grace, and how by the Spirit living within each believer the Law could be fulfilled on earth, as it is in heaven. This occurs with each Promise Seeking believer being filled with the Holy Spirit, growing in Spiritual Fitness, inheriting blessings of The Promise, and using those blessings to fight spiritual battles and bless others.

It is this growing in the Holy Spirit, by progressively inheriting the blessings of The Promise, that makes a Promise Seeking believer spiritually fit for the battle as a soldier of Faith. Expanding this allegory of the Apostle Paul, one must understand that being an ideal soldier does not mean just staying in the training camp; although, one's proper training is important. It does not mean marching in the parades; although, one has a right to be respected for their service. It does not mean socializing in the post clubs; although, one is entitled to rest after hard fatigue. Or, it is not attending the military ball in full dress uniform with metals showing; although, one can be rightly proud of one's heroics. No, that is not what it is about at all. It is about being on the battlefield, wading through the mud, enduring a cold night, vigilantly staying alert for the enemy, watching out for those in your company, persevering the boredom of waiting, staving off the fear, and being ready for engagement with all your skills at that moment the fight reaches you.

Promise Seeking believers need to understand that spiritual conflicts are fought out on the battlefields of life, where it is messy. Believers must be ready for that moment when the conflict reaches them, so they must be Spiritually Fit. Andrew Murray said that effectual Holy Spirit filled believers must learn well the lesson of the "first and the last". After Jesus had encountered the rich young ruler, He reassured his disciples of what was to come of those who sacrificed their lives for Him. Jesus said:

Matthew 19:29-30

> "And everyone who has left houses or brothers or sisters or father or mother or children or farms for My name's sake, shall receive many times as much, and shall inherit eternal life. But many who are first will be last and the last first." (NASB)

Becoming *Spiritually Fit* as a Promise Seeking believer is all about surrendering oneself, letting go of those ties that bind one to the world, and conquering one's lower nature; in order to develop "a polished ear" for the Holy Spirit. Since one's lower nature is set against the Spirit, it interferes with the Spirit's communication, and it must be put in check. Paul explained how Christ fulfilled the Law when he said:

Romans 8:4-5

> Therefore we are able to meet the Law's requirements, for we are living no longer by the dictates of our sinful nature, but in *obedience to the promptings of the Spirit.* The carnal man sees no further than carnal things, but the spiritual man is concerned with the things of the spirit. [69]

A primary key to becoming Spiritually Fit is focusing one's attention *away* from one's own desires and toward the needs of others, then stepping out in an act of Faith in accordance with "the promptings of the Spirit." One way to turn one's attention away from self is to search out some *conditional Scriptures* (Table III, Lesson 6) and practice them. Practice makes perfect, as they say, and everyone starts with little steps and gets better as they learn. Next, one can focus on others' needs by praying for those closest to them, or those in a Christian fellowship, fervently and earnestly in private. Next, listen to the Holy Spirit, so over time one can develop "a polished ear" for the "promptings of the Spirit". How does one hear God speak through the Holy Spirit? – likely a thousand different ways, for Jesus said to Nicodemus:

John 3:8

> "The wind blows where it wishes and you hear the sound of it, but do not know where it comes from and where it is going; so is everyone who is born of the Spirit." (NASB)

It is beyond words to explain how one hears "promptings" from the winds of the Holy Spirit, but those who are filled with the Holy Spirit and tap into His resources to do those things God calls upon them to do, certainly know of this Spirit and its power.

Obedience to Jesus' call to Spiritual Fitness

Jesus calls each individual believer to grow in Spiritual Fitness (i.e., Godliness and Holiness) through obedience to His Word. Peter wrote to Christians in Asia Minor:

I Peter 1:15-16

> – but like the Holy One who called you, be holy yourselves also in all *your* behavior; because it is written [in Lev. 20:7], "YOU SHALL BE HOLY, FOR I AM HOLY". (NASB)

Every Promise Seeking believer wishing to inherit blessings of The Promise by growing in Spiritual Fitness, must pick up his cross daily, follow Jesus, and abide by doing God's will (I John 2:16-17). Luke recorded Jesus' words:

Luke 9:23-24 (& Mark 8:34-35)

> And He was saying to them all, "If anyone wishes to come after Me, let him deny himself, and take up his cross daily, and follow Me. For whoever wishes to save his life shall lose it, but whoever loses his life for My sake, he is the one who will save it." (NASB)

No one needs to go out of his way to find his "daily cross". One does not need to go to the other side of the world; one does not need to look for another religious program; one does not need to find another community activity. No, Jesus has one's "daily cross" ready and waiting for each Promise Seeking believer. It could be a difficult, oppressive employment to do cheerfully. It could be a child to rear without spousal support or encouragement. It could be caring for an aging parent, who shows no gratitude or appreciation. It could be caring for a spouse during a protracted illness. It could be the unfortunate loss of a child. It could be some thankless duty to perform behind the scenes to the best of one's ability, as if only for Jesus. It could be a teacher who stays after class to spend her own time to help a struggling student, rather than allowing the child to be branded a non-achiever.

These are the "daily crosses" that one bears for Jesus. They fit into a global pattern for the good of ALL in the "body of Christ" that are so called to His purpose. One cannot see how they "fit" into God's plan anymore than a single soldier on a battlefield can tell how his fire-fight fits into the strategic plan of a large invasion force. Spiritual warfare involves fighting the battle presented to the Promise Seeking believer where he stands. He can be assured, if he is abiding by doing God's will, the spiritual battle will come to him; thus he is advised to be *Spiritually Fit* for the task. He need not be so prepared as to fight the entire battle alone or attempt to win the whole war. No, in practice, if he has sufficient *Spiritual Fitness*, and if he has learned how to release the power of the Holy Spirit by doing God's will; his task may not be nearly as difficult as he might anticipate.

A young child sitting in a class room struggling to read would never believe in his wildest imagination that some day he might be a university professor, but such is possible. It is equally so with spiritual growth and Spiritual Fitness: one starts out small, and as one grows in Godliness and Holiness by the power of the Holy Spirit; then greater things are possible, if one gets beyond the fundamentals and strives as a Promise Seeking believer. Remember what Jesus said:

Matthew 11:28-30

> "Come to Me, all who are weary and heavy-laden, and I will give you rest. Take My yoke upon you and learn from Me, for I am gentle and humble in heart; and YOU SHALL FIND REST FOR YOUR SOULS. For My yoke is easy, and My load is light." (NASB)

If one does not pay attention to developing *Spiritual Fitness*, the burden of one's cross might be difficult to bear, and the load might be heavy. But, with the power of the Holy Spirit the Promise Seeking believer by taking seriously *conditional* Scripture, by hearing the Word of Christ, by responding through acts of Faith, and by being obedient to Jesus' commandments will be prepared to meet the challenge of "his cross" with Inherited Blessings, accumulated through this iterative reinforcement of Faith and Obedience. As a result, he will find the "yoke" of Jesus easy and His "load" light on the chaotic battlefield of life.

ONE WHO GREW IN SPIRITUAL FITNESS

Life Group Meeting in late April 2013
Scripture: see List of Scripture

After our last Life Group meeting, I meditated on the theology that had unfolded before us. I had a sense that I had seen it before. Looking over my small bookcase of Christian books, I glanced at the classic Christian writers of the 20th century: J. B. Phillips, C. S. Lewis, Francis Schaeffer, etc. – Whose theology was this? Who had spoken about bearing one's cross, spiritual discipline, and suffering for Christ? Then it struck me. We had stumbled upon the theology of Dietrich Bonhoeffer. More correctly, the Holy Spirit had led us to Bonhoeffer's theology. Bonhoeffer's books were difficult to read, so most had remained on the shelf. Bonhoeffer's primary work was his 1937 book *Nachfolge*. I had its 1959 English translation: *The Cost of Discipleship* and its 2003 English translation: *Discipleship*. Reviewing these books, I saw a parallel between Bonhoeffer's beliefs and the theology we had uncovered. Bonhoeffer was a prime example of one who had matured in Faith by personal discipline and obedience.

The Faith and Obedience of Dietrich Bonhoeffer

In 1944, at the age of thirty-eight, a year before he was martyred, Dietrich Bonhoeffer reflected on a book he had written as a young theologian at the age of thirty-one. In seven years he had grown significantly in Spiritual Fitness. While in the Wehrmacht Interrogation Prison at Tegel in Berlin, for being implicated in a plot to assassinate Hitler, he wrote "I thought I could acquire faith by trying to live a holy life, or something like it. It was in this phase that I wrote 'The Cost of Discipleship'. Today I can see the dangers of this book, though, I am prepared to stand by what I wrote." [70] Subsequently, theologians would explain that, if Bonhoeffer had lived, he might have revised the book to show how Holiness (i.e., Spiritual Fitness & Godliness) is worked out in real practice by experience. He had matured in Godliness by being obedient to bearing his cross.

Having been reared by a devoted Christian mother in a well-to-do, aristocratic family, Bonhoeffer, at the age of fourteen, decided to be a theologian like his great-grandfather before him. He loved music, art, poetry, nature, and walking in the forest. An accomplished pianist and avid reader, everything came easy for Dietrich. Home-schooled along with his seven siblings by his mother and a governess until the age of eight, he gravitated towards all that was beautiful, good, and just. He enjoyed his close-knit loving family and extended relatives, all within a privileged environment of the exclusive, well-educated Grunewald neighborhood of Berlin. Although well schooled in the Christian faith at home, his family seldom attended church; for his father, a nationally prominent M.D. and professor of psychiatry and clinical neurology at the University of Berlin, was an agnostic.

Bonhoeffer advanced quickly, at a young age, to international prominence and became a lecturer of theology at the University of Berlin at the age of 25. Even though he lost his academic position for publicly opposing Hitler, he continued to teach, sometimes without pay, and traveled the globe giving lectures, serving churches, and attending ecumenical conferences. His early writings were very intellectual, often narrow in scope, and youthfully rebellious. Prior to his academic appointment in Berlin, during a year in New York as a post-graduate student, he experienced the spirit-filled Holiness of a large African-American congregation in Harlem, where he taught a children's Sunday school class. Years later, he recounted to a friend how that experience opened the Bible to him for the first time. He was personally "liberated" in what one could classify as a true "born-again" experience. Returning to Germany, friends and family would note that he was forever changed in his very personal commitment to Faith.

Although historians cannot establish the exact time of Bonhoeffer's conversion, it is presumed to have occurred in the United States between 1930-31, during one of the few times when he was alone and on his own. Bonhoeffer wrote in a letter of his spiritual awakening:

> Back then I was terribly alone and left to my own devices. It was quite awful. Then a change took place, a change that transformed my life and set its course in a new direction to this very day. I arrived at the Bible for the first time. Again, that is a terrible thing to admit. I had already preached quite often. I had seen much of the church, and both talked and written about it. But I had not yet become a Christian. In a wild and untamed way I was still my own master. ... In all my abandonment I was nevertheless quite pleased with myself. It was the Bible which liberated me from this, especially the Sermon on the Mount. Since then everything has changed. I could clearly feel it, and even other people around me noticed it. It was a great liberation. [71]

From then on Bonhoeffer would read the Bible with a quest to "enquire of it" personally for a Word from God. He would hold a passage in his mind for long periods, meditating on it for a message from God. Years later at a youth conference, on the isle of Fanø off the coast of Denmark, a participant recalled, "…Bonhoeffer reminded us that our primary object was not to commend our own views, national or individual, *but to hear what God would say to us*." [72] He would quote Psalm 85:8, "I will hear what God the Lord will speak: for he will speak peace unto his people, and to his saints: but let them not turn again to folly."

Bonhoeffer's earliest attempt at Holiness was to sequester himself within the fellowship of his students and colleagues by separating themselves from the world in an attempt to achieve Holiness (i.e., Spiritual Fitness & Godliness) by intellectual purification and prognostication; followed by protest, as opportunity provided. After realizing one must be "in" this world – but not "of" its evil – committed to caring for others in worldly situations by the power of the Holy Spirit for his faith to be real, he became involved in fighting the "good fight". He learned one must take an obedient stand before God to do "what is right" in all circumstances, regardless of the risk. Bonhoeffer exclaimed that living in the light of Christ's resurrection was the answer to Archimedes' query: "Give me somewhere to stand, and I will move the earth". He spoke out in sermons, lectures, letters and leaflets; working tirelessly to prevent the Nazi takeover of the German church. He secretly provided valuable information to governments opposing Hitler. He encouraged the international ecumenical movement to not shrink back from open confrontation with the emerging Nazi dominated Reichskirche. In a letter he wrote: "We must shake off our fear of this world – the cause of Christ is at stake, and are we to be found sleeping? … *Christ is looking down at us and asking whether there is anyone left who confesses faith in him*." [73]

In Christianity Today, Leonore Siegele-Wenschkewitz expressed the later years of Bonhoeffer's focus: "His prison letters, written during the last two years of his life, are perhaps the best-known of his works. He called for *mature*, credible Christian faith to be lived out in an increasingly secular, irreligious world." [74]

Bonhoeffer's letters from prison carried a different tone compared to his earlier academic treatises. His words carried a sense of sincere compassion and spiritual maturity. Stripped away was the intellectual philosophizing; left was a mature, warm-hearted, merciful compassion. One can surmise that he may not have truly known the meaning of "longsuffering" for Christ – aside from observing others –until he was arrested on April 5, 1943, because of his association with the Abwehr, which was implicated in a failed attempt on Hitler's life. Except for times abroad, and at Zingst and Finkenwalde with students of the new Confessing Church's illegal seminary, he had, for the most part, remained very connected to his loving family until his arrest. He knew that to grow in Godliness he had to be on the battlefield for Christ both spiritually and physically. By not staying abroad in America, he passed up a chance to save himself.

In later years, having failed at all collective approaches, he integrated himself into German Military Intelligence (i.e., the Abwehr, which was secretly opposed to the Nazi SS). His bother-in-law worked there, and with him Dietrich acted as a double agent, assisted the underground resistance, and smuggled Jews out of Germany.

Understanding that Bonhoeffer later admitted to some shortcomings in his book *The Cost of Discipleship*, if one reads it with an open mind and with solid biblical knowledge, one can grasp significant spiritual wisdom from his writing. First of all, in English the title is not well translated, for the book had little to do with salvation (which is free) or its cost (which was paid by Christ). The book is all about growth in Spiritual Fitness and Godliness, as one bears his cross.

The German title of Bonhoeffer's book was *Nachfolge*. Nach means "after"; folge means "succession"; and folger means "successor". There is no translation into German for the English word "discipleship", so it might not have been the best choice. The word "cost" likely should not have been added by English translators, because that was not the intended meaning. Nachfolge as a noun directly translates as "The Posting" or "The Post", or as a verb "To Post", as in a military assignment. So the meaning is about what one does *after* they have been selected as a *successor* to a position. In effect, how does one perform as did the forerunner, or the one previously in that position?

One may freely volunteer for military service, in particular the Special Forces, (that goes beyond the regular army), but one cannot choose "The Posting" to which he may be assigned on the battlefield. He must do his duty, and do his best to serve and to endure the consequences of "The Post". The same is true on the spiritual battlefield: a saved, "born-again" believer chooses to go beyond the fundamentals by growing in Spiritual Fitness to be ready for his assignment; then Christ, as the Supreme Commander, gives out one's cross, or "The Post", to which one is assigned on the spiritual battlefield. One is then "called" to "suffer" or "bear" his "cross" or "Post".

The title *Nachfolge* might have been better understood to mean: *The suffering one bears after answering the call of Christ to take up one's cross.* The book might have been better titled in English: The Suffering of Christ's Call to the Cross, or A Call to Suffer One's Cross, or just Suffering the Cross.

Listen to Bonhoeffer's words about the *cross* one bears from Chapter 4, entitled "Discipleship and the Cross". [75] :

> To deny oneself is to be aware of only Christ and no more self, to see only him who goes before and no more the road which is too hard for us.

To endure the cross is not a tragedy: it is the suffering which is the fruit of an exclusive allegiance to Jesus Christ. When it comes, it is not an accident, but a necessity.

The Psalmist was lamenting that he was despised and rejected of men, and that is an essential quality of the suffering of the cross.

Only a man thus totally committed in discipleship can experience the meaning of the cross. The cross is there, right from the beginning, he has only to pick it up: there is no need for him to go out and look for a cross for himself, no need for him deliberately to run after suffering. Jesus says that every Christian has his own cross waiting for him, a cross destined and appointed by God.

The passion of Christ strengthens him to overcome the sins of others by forgiving them. He becomes the bearer of other men's burdens – "Bear ye one another's burdens, and so fulfill the law of Christ. (Gal.6:2)"

Suffering, then is the badge of true discipleship.

Suffering is the badge of a wholeheartedly genuine follower of Christ, but that badge is sown to the *inside* pocket of one's coat.

Bonhoeffer also understood the interaction between acting on faith and obedience to God's will in building Spiritual Fitness. Bonhoeffer admitted that he could not "acquire faith" by attempting to "live a Holy life". He incorrectly thought obedience came FIRST before faith. He later learned it was the other way around. He surely would have changed his thinking after years of reflection and experience, for scripture states faith comes by *hearing* and obedience follows. This is seen by what Paul said to the Romans in 10:17: "So faith comes from hearing, and hearing by the Word of Christ." (NASB)

However, Bonhoeffer did understand that faith and obedience were mutually reinforcing of each other in building Spiritual Fitness. Listen to his words about *obedience* to the *cross* from Chapter 2 entitled "The Call to Discipleship": [76]

The road to faith passes through obedience to the call of Jesus. Unless a definite step is demanded, the call vanishes into thin air, and if men imagine that they can follow Jesus without taking this step, they are deluding themselves like fanatics.

Only he who believes is obedient, and only he who is obedient believes.

For faith is **only real** when there is obedience, never without it, and faith only becomes [real] faith in the act of obedience.

In the one case faith is the condition for obedience, and in the other obedience the condition of faith.

Only the obedient believe. If we are to believe, we must obey a concrete command. …. The commandment may be variously interpreted, and it is God's will that it should be interpreted and explained: for God has given man a *free-will* to decide what he will do.

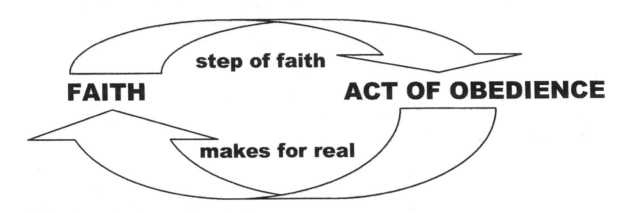

To love Jesus *requires obedience* to His three direct commandments, as well as all His other *conditional* statements provided to help one understand how to exhibit Christ's extraordinary love in fulfillment of the Spirit of the Law (see Tables III and the Spiritual Fitness Inventory in Lesson 9 with interpretation open to the believer). One must never forget what Jesus said:

John 14:21

> "He who has My commandments and **keeps them**, he it is who loves Me; and he who loves me shall be loved by My Father, and I will love him, and will disclose Myself to him." (NASB)

Bonhoeffer emphasizes obedience to Jesus' commandments when he writes:

> No one should be surprised at the difficulty of faith [or spiritual growth], if there is some part of his life [where he is] disobeying the commandment of Jesus. Is there some part of your life which you are refusing to surrender at his behest, some sinful passion, maybe, or some animosity, some hope, perhaps your ambition or your reason? If so, you must not be surprised that you have not received the Holy Spirit [or have not learned to release its power], that prayer is difficult, or that your request for faith [or opportunity for spiritual growth] remains unanswered. [77]

A year before being arrested, Bonhoeffer wrote, and hid, an essay succinctly assessing ten years of his struggle under the Third Reich. The essay enunciated the deception of evil, the "cheap grace" of religion, and the maturity of responsible faith:

> The great masquerade of evil has played havoc with all our ethical concepts. For evil to appear disguised as light, charity, historical necessity, or social justice is quite bewildering to anyone brought up on our traditional ethical concepts, while for the Christian who bases his life on the Bible it merely confirms the fundamental wickedness of evil. ... Who stands fast? Only the man whose final standard is not his reason, his principles, his conscience, his freedom, or his virtue, but who is ready to sacrifice all this when he is call to *obedient* and *responsible action* in faith and in exclusive allegiance to God – the responsible man, who tries to make his whole life an answer to *the question* and *call of God.* Where are these responsible people? [78]

Eric Metaxas, in his superbly written biography of Bonhoeffer, boldly and frankly summarized the assessment: "This was how Bonhoeffer saw what he was doing. He had theologically redefined the Christian life as something active, not reactive. ... It had everything to do with living one's whole life in obedience to God's call through *action.* It did not merely require a mind, but a body too. It was God's call to be fully human, to live as human beings obedient to the one who has made us, which was the fulfillment of our destiny. It was not a cramped, compromised, circumspect life, but a life lived in a kind of wild, joyful, full-throated freedom – that was what it was to obey God." [79]

After nearly sixteen months in Tegel prison at Seidelstrasse 39, Berlin, on July 21, 1944, Bonhoeffer writes to Eberhard Bethge about "living completely in this world":

> During the last year or so I've come to know and understand more and more the profound this-worldliness of Christianity. The Christian is not a *homo religiosus,* but simply a man, as Jesus was a man – in contrast, shall we say, to John the Baptist. I don't mean the shallow and banal this-worldliness of the enlightened, the busy, the comfortable, or the lascivious, but the profound this-worldliness, characterized by discipline and the constant knowledge of death and resurrection. I think Luther lived a this-worldly life in this sense.
>
> I remember a conversation that I had in America thirteen years ago with a young French pastor. We were asking ourselves quite simply what we wanted to do with our lives. He said he would like to become a saint (and I think it's quite likely that he did become one). At the time I was very impressed, but I disagreed with him, and said, in effect, that I should like to have faith. For a long time I didn't realize the depth of the contrast. I thought I could acquire faith by trying to live a holy life, or something like it. I suppose I wrote *The*

> *Cost of Discipleship* at the end of that path. Today I can see the dangers of that book, though I still stand by what I wrote.
>
> I discovered later, and I'm still discovering right up to this moment, that is it only by **living completely in this world** that one learns to have faith. One must completely abandon any attempt to make something of oneself, whether it be a saint, or a converted sinner, or a churchman (a so-called priestly type!), a righteous man or an unrighteous one, a sick man or a healthy one. By this-worldliness I mean living unreservedly in life's duties, problems, successes and failures, experiences and perplexities. In so doing we throw ourselves completely into the arms of God, taking seriously not our own sufferings, but those of God in the world – watching with Christ in Gethsemane. That, I think, is faith; that is *metanoia* [repentance], and that is how one becomes a man and a Christian (cf. Jer.45!). How can success make us arrogant, or failure lead us astray, when we share in God's sufferings through a life of this kind?
>
> I think you see what I mean, even though I put it so briefly, I'm glad to have been able to learn this, and I know I've been able to do so along the road that I've travelled. So I'm grateful for the past and present and content with them. [80]

The key passage in Jeremiah 45 is the last verse where God speaks: " 'And seekest thou great things for thyself? – seek *them* not: for, behold, I will bring evil upon all flesh', saith the Lord: 'but *thy life* will I give unto *thee* for a prey in all places whither thou goest.' " (KJV) This means that God gives each believer a life to be used by one's personal *free-will* choices as a sacrifice to either glorify God or oneself. (More details regarding Bonhoeffer's theology are given in Appendix II.)

In a letter to his fiancée Maria, just three and a half months before his death, he said: "… you mustn't think I'm unhappy. Anyway, what do happiness and unhappiness mean? They depend so little on circumstances and so much more on what goes on inside us. I'm thankful every day to have – you and all of you – and that makes me happy and cheerful." [81]

Maria's cousin Fabian von Schlarendorff, who survived the war, was at the time a fellow prisoner with Bonhoeffer. Later he recounted Dietrich's optimistic attitude: "It was significant for our relationship that he was rather the hopeful one while I now and then suffered from depressions. He always cheered me up and comforted me, he never tired of repeating that the only fight which is lost is that which we give up. Many little notes he slipped into my hands on which he had written biblical words of comfort and hope." [82]

After two years in prison Bonhoeffer was executed on April 9, 1945. The camp doctor, H. Fischer-Hüllstrung, witnessed the execution. He later remembered: "I saw Pastor Bonhoeffer kneeling on the floor praying fervently to God. I was most deeply moved by the way this lovable man prayed, so devout and so certain that God heard his prayer. At the place of execution, he again said a short prayer and then climbed the few steps to the gallows, brave and composed. His death ensued after a few seconds. In the almost fifty years that I worked as a doctor, I have hardly ever seen a man die so entirely submissive to the will of God." [83]

On July 27, 1945, a memorial service was conducted in England to honor Bonhoeffer. Sabine, Bonhoeffer's twin sister, with her husband Gerhard Leibholz united with Franz Hildebrandt at Holy Trinity Brompton to remember Dietrich. Gathered were close friends, ecumenical associates, and some congregation members from the two German pastorates Bonhoeffer serviced for two years soon after receiving his doctorate. Franz Hildebrandt had been one of Bonhoeffer's closest friends. He knew Dietrich in the early years, before seeking refuge in England because of his Jewish heritage; as did Sabine's husband for the same reason. Hildebrandt, a Christian minister, delivered one of the eulogies, which reflected on Bonhoeffer's extraordinary spiritual growth over roughly a decade, from the time of his spiritual awakening, after his first trip to American up to the time they lost contact.

> – from the agonizing quest to the confident discipleship lies the secret of Dietrich Bonhoeffer and his legacy for us. One can study it from the development of his style; from the earliest abstract analyses to the last pages of the *Cost of Discipleship* it grows more and more simple and unburdened. A reviewer of *Creation and Fall* writes: "there is more in these hundred pages than in many a theological tome; every word is weighed and every sentence fits." It was not different with his life. The yoke he took was easy, and the burden of his master light; the vision cleared as he looked to Jesus, away from himself, and what a year ago he had written of the Christian's hope [that] was now fulfilled: He becomes what he was – or rather, never was – a child. [84]

Bonhoeffer's growth in Spiritual Fitness was phenomenal. Witnesses to his later years under extremely horrid captivity attest to his calm, fearless, up-lifting nature. Assuredly, he carried his cross with joyful confidence. He had inherited so many blessings of The Promise, that, indeed, his yoke had become easy and his burden light by releasing enormous spiritual strength of the Holy Spirit. He remained a child at heart, but became a giant of a man in spiritual discipline and Godliness.

Obedience to Christ

Obedience to Christ means the Promise Seeking believer MUST DO SOMETHING in the way of Jesus' *conditional* commandments to get beyond the fundamentals and to answer the call to Spiritual Fitness and Godliness, if one is to endure one's cross with ease, as claimed in Matt.11:30.

Obedience to Christ is abiding by doing God's will over and over again (I John 2:17), thus strengthening one's faith and obedience *iteratively* with each experience, as one builds Spiritual Fitness. A lifestyle of abiding by faith and obedience to God's will follows action steps that:

hear the Word of Christ → **deny** self → **pray** in ALL things → **listen** to Holy Spirit → **act** on Faith → **care** for others→ **suffer** as Christ → **wait** on God → **inherit** blessing.

Abide by repeating, over and over again, this self-subordinating lifestyle cycle of being obedient to God's will; in order to more easily release the power of the Holy Spirit, thus becoming more Spiritually Fit and growing in Godliness with each Inherited Blessing.

Take Time to be Holy [85]
William D. Longstaff (1822-1894)

Take time to be Holy. – Speak oft with the Lord;
Abide in Him always, – And feed on His Word.
Make friends with God's children; – Help those who are weak,
Forgetting in nothing – His blessing to seek.

Take time to be Holy. – The world rushes on;
Spend much time in secret – With Jesus alone.
By looking to Jesus, – Like Him thou shalt be;
Thy friends in thy conduct – His likeness shall see.

Take time to be Holy. – Let Him be thy Guide;
And run not before Him, – Whatever betide.
In joy or in sorrow, – Still follow thy Lord
And, looking to Jesus, – Still trust in His Word.

A SPIRITUAL FITNESS INVENTORY

A part of the Life Group Meeting in late April 2013
Scripture: Romans 12:9-21 & Passages in Inventory

Glorify Christ with Genuine Christian Behavior

The ultimate purpose of a believer growing in Spiritual Fitness and Godliness is to glorify Christ by using one's Inherited Blessings of the Holy Spirit. The importance of privacy and secret deeds of mercy is so that *only* one's Christ-like integrity is seen by the world. The actual deeds of obedience and growing in Spiritual Fitness ARE NOT for the purpose of building one's reputation – that is the wrong reason.

One should never forget the line from T. S. Eliot's play, "Murder in the Cathedral", which depicted the true story of Archbishop Thomas Becket's execution by the King's knights in 1170. Becket, knowing his martyrdom was eminent, said to the fourth tempter, who encouraged him to glorify himself:

> Now is my way clear, now is the meaning plain:
> Temptation shall not come in this kind again.
> The last temptation is *the greatest treason:*
> *To do the right deed for the wrong reason.*

The Promise Seeking believer grows in Spiritual Fitness, and, in doing so, exhibits genuine Christian behavior as an outgrowth of the Godliness in his mature Faith. This mature, wholeheartedly genuine Christian behavior is best summarized by the Apostle Paul in Romans Chapter 12.

Romans 12:9-21

> Let us have no imitation Christian Love. Let us have a genuine hatred for evil and a real devotion to good. Let us have a real warm affection for one another as between brothers, and a willingness to let the other man have the credit. Let us not allow slackness to spoil our work and let us keep the fires of the spirit

burning, as we do our work for the Lord. Base your happiness on your hope in Christ. When trials come endure them patiently; steadfastly maintaining a habit of prayer. Give freely to fellow Christians in want, never grudging a meal or a bed to those who need them. And as for those who try to make your life a misery, bless them. Don't curse, bless. Share the happiness of those who are happy and the sorrow of those who are sad. Live in harmony with each other. Don't become snobbish but take a real interest in ordinary people. Don't become set in you own opinions. Don't pay back a bad turn by a bad turn, to anyone. See that your public behavior is above criticism. As far as your responsibility goes, live at peace with everyone. Never take vengeance into your own hands, my dear friends: stand back and let God punish if he will. For it is written: 'Vengeance belongeth unto me: I will recompense, saith the Lord.' And it is also written: 'If thine enemy hunger, feed him; If he thirst, give him drink; For in so doing thou shalt heap coals of fire upon his head.' *Don't allow yourself to be overpowered by evil. Take the offensive – overpower evil with good!* [86]

Assessing the State of One's Spiritual Fitness by Inventory

Following Bonhoeffer's suggestion that each Promise Seeking believer has the God given *free-will* to interpret and explain Jesus' commandments for himself, it is beneficial for one to assess one's own Christ-like character against the state of their Spiritual Fitness. To do this, a Promise Seeker's Spiritual Fitness Christ-like Character Inventory has been created below. Each believer – alone in the privacy of their own "prayer closet" – should read each **Word of Christ Attribute** stated by Jesus, and then read the corresponding challenge questions, or directives implied by the Word of Christ, in order to fulfill the Spirit of the Law through the Holy Spirit's extraordinary Christ-like behavior.

The Promise Seeker's Spiritual Fitness
Christ-Like Character Inventory

How much does one *focus* on the Word of Christ to build Spiritual Fitness through acting on Faith and being obedient to suffering the cross Christ calls one to bear? Remember what Paul said: "Faith comes from hearing, and hearing by the Word of Christ." (Rom. 10:17) Promise Seeking believers need to reflect on their spiritual maturity by answering the questions found in the Spiritual Fitness Inventory given in Table V.

T. C. PINKERTON

Table V – Spiritual Fitness Christ-Like Character Inventory

	Word of Christ Attribute	Go Beyond the Fundamentals
The Word of Christ as Direct Commandments that Sum Up the Spirit of the Law		
1	Love God with all your heart, mind, soul, and strength.*	Do you apply Jesus' love definitions to God?
2	Care for your neighbors as yourself with brotherly love.*	Do you love you enemies as well?
The Word of Christ as a "New Commandment" to Care for the Closest as did Jesus		
3	Care for the closest to you with self-sacrificing love.	Do you sacrifice yourself to your family and to your companions in Christ?
Jesus Spoke to Eight (*) of the Law's Commandments (Matthew Chapter 5)		
4	Honor your father & mother.*	Do you care for your parents and speak well of them?
5	You shall not murder.*	Are you easily angered? Do you belittle others or discourage them with unnecessary criticism or empty speech?
6	You shall not commit adultery.*	Are you faithful in all things? Can you be trusted?
7	You shall not steal.*	Are you always honest? Do you give others more than they ask for? Do you go the extra mile?
8	You shall not lie.*	How honest are you? Do you hide some truth?
9	You shall not covet.*	Do you desire more than you need? How thankful are you for what you have? Do you give more when asked for a little?
The Remaining Four of the Ten Commandments		
10	You shall have no gods before Me.	How many worldly things do you worship?
11	You shall have no idols before you.	What worldly things do you idolize?

94

12	You shall not use the Lord's name in vain.	How vain or frivolous is your language?
13	Remember the Sabbath and keep it Holy.	Do you honor God at least one day a week?

The Word of Christ in the Beatitudes (Matthew Chapter 5)

14	Blessings as heirs to heaven	Do you think about your spiritual poverty?
15	Blessings of God's comfort	Have you experienced undeserved sorrow?
16	Blessings as "Salt of Earth"	Have you been gentle and humble?
17	Blessings of a satisfied spirit	Do you hunger and thirst for true righteousness?
18	Blessings of God's mercy	Have you shown mercy to others?
19	Blessings as Sons of God	Have you tried to make peace in all situations?
20	Great rewards in heaven	Have you been insulted, slandered, or persecuted for doing "what is right" before God for Christ's sake?

The Word of Christ in the Definition of Agape Love (I Corinthians Chapter 13)

21	Love is slow to lose patience.	Are you patient in all circumstances?
22	Love is constructive.	Do you always try to be kind and helpful?
23	Love is not possessive.	How eager are you to let go of control?
24	Love does not impress or brag.	Are you too concerned about your importance?
25	Love does not inflate oneself.	Are you realistic about your capabilities?
26	Love has good manners.	Are you always polite to others?
27	Love does not pursue gain.	Do you seek selfish advantage?
28	Love is not easily provoked.	Are you always on-edge or touchy?
29	Love does not keep account of evil.	Do you keep track of others' wrong doings?
30	Love does not gloat over wickedness of others.	Do you get self-satisfaction in pointing out the unrighteousness of others?
31	Love rejoices with the truth.	Do you support those who stand-up for truth?
32	Love has no limits to its endurance.	Do you endure all the circumstances and situations in which God places you?

33	Love has no end to its trust.	Do you trust by always doing "what is right"?
34	Love has no fading of its hope.	Do you stay positive in all circumstances?
35	Love can outlast anything.	Do you wait on God with perseverance?
36	Love never fails.	Do you never fail those God brings to you?

The Word of Christ in Taking Action (Matthew 7:7 & John 10:10)		
37	Recognize your need for God's help in living an "abundant" life.	In all things do you **ask** for help in prayer, **seek** answers from God, and **knock** on doors to find opportunities?

The Word of Christ in Praise (Philippians 4:6-7)		
38	Pray and be thankful in all things.	In everything do you give prayerful praise and thanksgiving to God?

The Word of Christ in Doing God's Will (Hebrews 6:19)		
39	Anchor your hope in steadfastly doing God's will.	Do you search your heart to determine if your motivations are truly aligned with God's will for each circumstance?

The Word of Christ in Forgiveness (Matthew 6:14)		
40	Forgive others in all transgressions.	Do you have a forgiving spirit? Do you truly repent and ask God to forgive you of all your transgressions?

The Word of Christ in Defending the Faith (Ephesians 6:10-18)		
41	Stand firm against evil.	Do you always stand up against wrong doing?
42	Hold to the truth.	Do you stand on truth of the Gospel, even when it is not popular?
43	Endure righteousness.	Do you do "what is right", even when it may get you in trouble?
44	Make peace with everyone.	Before you venture out, do you consciously plan to be at peace with those you encounter? Do you help others with inner peace?

45	Have faith in God's ways.	Do you honestly use good deeds against evil, or do you defend yourself with skills from human nature?
46	Discern the Word of God.	Do you truly strive to understand the Word of God and actually integrate the meaning of God's spiritual message into every thought, so that your salvation produces a sound mind ready to fend off evil?
47	Pray in the Spirit.	Do you pray in all things by the Spirit and let the Holy Spirit pray for you when you cannot pray in accordance with God's will?
48	Focus on others' need for prayer.	Are you always on the alert to see the prayer needs of others, to apply petitions of prayer, and to persevere in that prayer?
The Word of Christ in Prayer (Romans 12:12)		
49	Maintain a habit of prayer.	Do you endure trials patiently with a steadfast persistence in earnest prayer, or do you seek a way out of a circumstance?
A Word of Christ to a Humble Private Righteousness (Matthew 6:1-6)		
50	Do your deeds in secret.	Do you do your good deeds so everyone can see them, or do you do God's will so only He sees it? Are you always grandstanding, or do you let your actions speak louder than your words?
51	Do your prayer in private.	Are you always praying where someone can take notice of you, or do you reserve your earnest, fervent prayer for your private sanctuary?
52	Build up your treasure in heaven.	Do you build up treasures in heaven, or do you build up your reputation in your local religious organization or among your fellow believers? Do you forfeit your rewards in heaven by bragging about what you have done? Are you truly focused on heaven?

STUDY CONCLUSION

Jesus' active ministry on earth happened in roughly three years. In that time, he gathered only a handful of close associates (the disciples), most of whom he sent out on missions. Although Jesus knew everything about anyone he met, most of his encounters were brief exchanges with individuals that today one would call "strangers". Jesus did not spend most of his time gathered together with his disciples in a closed social community, monastically concerned for their own well-being. No, he pulled his disciples away from their friends and family, and asked them to give up everything (Matt. 19:29-30) and follow him. He spent most of his time doing the work of His Father on the road of life, sacrificing himself to ANYONE who would listen – without pretense. The only persons to raise Jesus' Holy anger were the leaders of the Old Covenant, who were more concerned with regulating religion than truly caring for the souls of their following.

In two thousand years some things have not changed. Multitudes try to grow in Godliness by being religious without obedience to their cross. Others want endless church programs. Some focus only on the well-being of Christian friends they've known for years. Many lay over and over again the fundamentals, as if they have yet to grasp them. A few repetitiously recite Bible passages without living their meaning. Irrespective of how sincere the efforts may be, all risk missing out on the Inherited Blessings of The Promise.

No, one must **get beyond the fundamentals** of the Faith and move on to

- BUILDING SPIRITUAL FITNESS,
- LISTENING TO THE PROMPTINGS OF THE HOLY SPIRIT,
- LIVING THE SCRIPTURE BY ACTS OF FAITH WITH OBEDIENCE TO SUFFERING ONE'S CROSS, AND
- INHERITING BLESSINGS OF THE PROMISE, SO THEY MAY RUN THE GOOD RACE AND FIGHT THE GOOD FIGHT TO GLORIFY JESUS.

Promise Seeking believers are called to focus on the Cross of Christ, as it has been assigned to them. With His sacrificial love they will build Spiritual Fitness through the power of the Holy Spirit and inherit blessings for use in this world and the next.

T. C. PINKERTON

Being a Promise Seeking believer is not so much about caring for those who love you; although, that is a part of Jesus' "new commandment". No, it is more about sacrificing oneself in genuine Christ-like love, made Spiritually Fit by the power of the Holy Spirit through patiently enduing "longsuffering"; so that the believer can love with humility ANYONE whom God brings across his path.

This study may be closed by recalling Jesus' final words in Matthew Chapter 5:

Matthew 5:43-48

> "You have heard that it used to be said, 'Thou shall love thy neighbor, and hate thine enemy', but I tell you, 'Love your enemies, and pray for those who persecute you', so that you may be sons of your Heavenly Father. For he makes his sun rise upon evil men as well as good, and he sends his rain upon the honest and dishonest men alike. For if you love only those who love you, what credit is that to you? Even the tax-collectors do that! And if you exchange greetings only with your own circle, are you doing anything exceptional? Even the pagans do that much. No, you will be perfect as your Heavenly Father is perfect." [87]

If believers are wholeheartedly genuine in their faithful obedience to Spiritually Fit Godliness to those outside their circle by the power of the Holy Spirit when their crosses are borne by suffering, then they will inherit blessings of The Promise with which they may humbly exhibit the perfection of God.

And, when believers ultimately stand before God, they will be clothed in the true righteousness of their secret heavenly treasures. They will stand alone to collect their reward, not with their friends by their side to advocate rewards by glowing accounts of impressive observed deeds.

With only the secrets of their Godly character as their clothing, with the cross of suffering sown to an inside pocket, where even the believer cannot see, they will face Christ.

Bonhoeffer summarizes:

> God alone knows our good works, while we know only God's good work and listen to God's command. We journey under God's grace, we walk in God's commandments, and we sin. There is indeed no denying the fact that the new righteousness, the sanctification, the light which ought to shine remains completely hidden from us. The left hand does not know what the right hand is doing. But we have faith and trust that "the one who began the good work in us" will bring it to completion by the day of Jesus Christ (Phil.1:6). On that day, Jesus Christ himself will reveal to us the good works of which we had

100

been unaware. Without knowing it, we have fed him, provided him with drink, given him clothes, and visited him; and without knowing it, we have turned him away. On that day, we will be greatly astonished, and we will recognize that it is not our works which endure here but the work which God, in God's own time, accomplished through us without our intention and effort (Matt. 25:31). Once again, the only thing left for us is to look away from ourselves and to look to the one who has already accomplished everything for us, and to follow this one. [88]

The ultimate goal of growing in Spiritual Fitness is to "look away from ourselves." As we dedicate ourselves to a lifestyle of doing God's will by abiding, through hearing the Word of Christ, denying self, praying in all things, listening to the Holy Spirit, acting on Faith, caring for others, suffering as did Christ, waiting on God, and inheriting blessings; we progressively turn more and more away from ourselves, until our actions of caring for others become more and more innate, second nature, and even unconscious to us, as God takes over with His work "in us".

One's Godly character has matured. Annealed under fire on the battlefield of a "calling", a Faith has been obedient to His will. God has sanctified another soul, who has surrendered to His hand. God's work is finished. Heaven awaits.

FIVE GROUPS WITH CHARACTERISTICS STATED IN PARALLEL

One can recognize distinct fundamental differences between a mature Christian, an immature Christian, a "backsliding" Christian, a "fallen away" Christian (who has committed a sin against the Holy Spirit), and an unsaved non-Christian. Here are twelve key characteristics restated in parallel.

Mature Christian

- saved - believes in heart and confesses with mouth (Romans 10:9-10)
- forgiven – acknowledges each sin, repents, and asks for forgiveness
- faith – strong underlining foundation of faith; makes large faith decisions
- crucified self – "gotten rid of his worst enemy" – self
- honors God in all things, fully committed – Christ's 1st commandment
- cares for others over self – Christ's 2nd commandment
- prepared to sacrifice self – Christ's 3rd commandment
- surrendered – completely given over to Holy Spirit within
- integrity – high moral standard; transparent; honest with self and others
- listens to God – knows how to "hear" God "speak" through Holy Spirit
- blessings – fruits of Holy Spirit, strong prayer life, experiences miracles
- heaven bound – focus, hope, and rewards on eternal life with Christ

Immature Christian

- saved - believes in heart and confesses with mouth (Romans 10:9-10)
- forgiven – generally acknowledges sin and asks for forgiveness
- faith – cannot get beyond foundation; makes only little faith decisions
- holds onto self - not completely given up self, so still vulnerable to World
- honors God in some things, but not fully committed
- cares for others as it satisfies needs of self
- not prepared to sacrifice self in real-world; depends on other Christians

- not surrendered to Holy Spirit – holds to religious myths & rituals of past
- integrity – moderate moral standard; not entirely honest with self or others
- weak divine listening skills - cannot discern a message from Holy Spirit
- blessings – some fruits of Holy Spirit, weak prayer life, few miracles
- heaven can wait – primarily focused on rewards of life on earth

A "backsliding" Christian (salvation not lost)

- saved - believes in heart and confesses with mouth (Romans 10:9-10)
- forgiven – likely not asking forgiveness for each sin; unrepentant
- returned to satisfying self, but not completely taken back in by The World
- honors God in some behavior, speech, or actions
- cares for self and others, but drifting away from caring for others
- would likely not sacrifice self except under extreme circumstances
- may have once known Holy Spirit, but not allowing Holy Spirit to guide life
- integrity – compromising standards; developing a double life
- partially listens to God and does God's will sometimes as convenient
- missing blessings – fruits of Spirit limited, no prayer life, no miracles
- heaven forgotten – turned attention to worldly pleasures

A Former Christian who committed the "unpardonable" sin

- once saved - believed in heart and confessed with mouth
- once forgiven, but stopped acknowledging sins and asking for forgiveness
- faith abandon – makes no faith decisions; relies only on what is seen
- returned to satisfying self and taken back in by The World
- no longer honors God in behavior, speech, or actions
- cares for self more than others
- would not sacrifice self under any circumstance
- **once knew Holy Spirit**, but consciously turned against Holy Spirit because could not use the power of Holy Spirit to satisfy self
- low integrity, not trustworthy; outer-self "looks good", but inner-self vengeful
- no longer listens to God's will, and is actively working against God's will
- no blessings – intentionally with malice of forethought blasphemed against and attacked the Holy Spirit in public, so committed the unforgivable sin – remains eternally outside of God's grace
- against heaven – hell bound and boasting about it

A non-Christian with potential for salvation (heart still has "soft spot")

- unsaved – does not believe, but salvation is available regardless of sin
- not forgiven – but forgiveness available

- faith faculty not yet discovered – lives by human instincts and judgment
- lives life by edicts of human nature to satisfy self interests
- does not honor God in all things, but may in some things
- cares for others as it suits self interest
- could sacrifice self, if it met a need to satisfy pride in something
- holds onto self – security in present; cannot yet "know" Holy Spirit
- integrity strained – may be respectable, but his conscience bothers him
- may see God in nature or people, but messages from God perplexing
- blessings or miracles interpreted as coincidences; may "pray" to anything, particularly in time of danger or severe need
- unsure of heaven – has 50:50 bet on heaven; may help people under a false hope of favoring the odds

APPENDIX II

AN ASSESSMENT OF DIETRICH BONHOEFFER'S THEOLOGY BASED ON HIS BOOK: *DISCIPLESHIP*

Bonhoeffer's theology is based on a very personal, modest, and unpretentious faith that cannot be defined "as doctrine, as principle, as system", but is "to be lived out in the midst of the world" in "simple obedience" to Jesus' commandments, emulated by the Sermon on the Mount. An individual must seek God's "costly grace" in all "situations" by humbly bearing a "hidden" cross of "suffering" in loving self-sacrificial defense of anyone who is burdened or oppressed by the evils of the world. The theology has a solid biblical foundation. It is well balanced between synoptic proclamations and Paul's Christ "in us" pronouncements. It is a full-gospel theology, which embraces all Jews as God's people, as well as those spiritually within the promise of Abraham through Christ. The theology places a strong emphasis on one bearing a particular "cross", which Christ assigns to that person. The theology is very individualistic, for a **personal decision** is necessary to see and to pick up one's cross. The "church" is not any type of human organization, but a community-brotherhood (Nachfolgemeinde) of dispersed souls who declare belief, accept baptism, bear a "cross", follow God's Word, renew sacraments, and commune with those "in Christ". One's faith is **only** made real by action and is most powerful when risking self to save others from evil. Suffering for Christ is necessary to grow in Holiness for sanctification. Some attributes of Bonhoeffer's theology are as follows:

- The Bible is the Word of God that "speaks" to each individual personally, if he accepts the Holy Spirit within himself by an awakening to the realization of Christ "in us". *One must individually know and follow Jesus' commandments.*

- Although one can accept Christ, be baptized, and mentally understand the Gospel; one does not begin to grow in Christ spiritually and become alive "in Christ" until one recognizes and "alone" **decides** to pick up one's cross daily.

- Once "in Christ" one can only relate or truly connect to other individuals through Christ as the mediator (i.e., the High Priest in heaven). Building one's relationship with Christ enables one to divinely connect with others. Attempts to establish a worldly relationship, by conforming to the ways of the world, by using human psychology, or by employing sociopolitical instincts, is no longer possible except with strain, falsehood, and hypocrisy. One must **live** the Sermon on the Mount.

- The "body of Christ" is a brotherhood of all who are "in Christ", who are growing in the Holy Spirit, who pick up their cross daily, and who connect to others **only** through Christ. The "body of Christ" makes up the living Christ on earth today. Those "in Christ" accept and relate with each other innately. Those not "in Christ" but with an open heart will listen and associate with those "in Christ" out of curiosity, or a desire to know God. Those opposed to Christ will **reject** and **persecute** those "in Christ", who by suffering such treatment become "new human beings".

- One's character and demeanor identifies them as being "in Christ", not their continued proclamation, or good intentioned activities, or membership in a religious group. One who is fully "in Christ" *does not see the Holiness of God in himself*; he only sees the sin in himself, for he is focused entirely on others. The progressive denying of oneself and growing in Holiness is sanctification.

- One "in Christ" will *of necessity* **suffer** the *rejection and persecution* of those not "in Christ" as a continued crucifixion of Christ on earth. Christ's death on the cross atoned for original sin and enabled salvation for all by God's "costly grace", but some "in Christ" must be martyred, as a part of the living Christ's "unfinished" work (Col. 1:24), in order to bear the on-going transgressions of Christians.

LIST OF SCRIPTURE

The following are passages either quoted or referenced. They are listed as they appear in the text, thus some are repeated from Lesson to Lesson. Multiple passages in the text are listed together.

Lesson 1

Philippians 3:12-16, Hebrews 6:1-3, Hebrews 4:12, II Corinthians 10:3-5, Psalms 91:1, Philippians 4:8, II Timothy 3:15

Lesson 2

Hebrews 6:4-8, Mark 3:28-30, Matthew 12:30-32, Matthew 10:33, Romans 10:9-10, Matthew 16:16, Matthew 16:23, Romans 1:28-29, Galatians 1:6-10, II Peter 1:4-8, Matthew 13:1-23, Matthew 6:14-15

Lesson 3

Hebrews 6:9-12, Hebrews 3:6, 3:14, 4:11 & 6:11, Philippians 3:8-12, John 13:34-35, John 15:7-8, John 15:12-15, John 15:11, Hebrews 11:13, Hebrews 11:39-40, Galatians 2:20

Lesson 4

Hebrews 6:13-15, Hebrews 11:1 & 11:6, Isaiah 40:28-31, Luke 9:23, Hebrews 10:36, John 15:18, Genesis 1:22, 1:28 & 9:1, Matthew 6:14-15, Revelation 3:19, Ephesians 4:12-16, I Corinthians 13:11-13 & 13:4-8, I Corinthians 14:20, Mark 10:25, Matthew 7:14, Matthew 5:16, Matthew 10:38-39, Matthew 20:20-28

Lesson 5

Hebrews 6:16-20, I Samuel 2:30, Hebrews 11:1, Hebrews 10:36, II Thessalonians 3:10, Hebrews 6:20, Ruth 1:16

T. C. PINKERTON

Lesson 6

John 14:21, Luke 23:42-43, (see Table II), I Thessalonians 2:9, II Timothy 2:2-6, Proverbs 14:23, 12:27 & 18:9, Hebrews 6:12, II Peter 1:5-6, James 5:11, I Timothy 4:8, II Timothy 2:1-6, Ephesians 6:12, II Corinthians 10:3-4, II Timothy 1:7, Matthew 6:1-6, Matthew 6:16-18, Matthew 6:19-21, Romans 8:28, (see Table III)

Lesson 7

I Corinthians 14:20, I Corinthians 13:11-12, I Timothy 4:7-8, Ephesians 6:10-18, I Corinthians 13:3-7, Galatians 5:22-25, Ephesians 5:4, Hebrews 6:1-3, Romans 8:4, Romans 8:23, Romans 8:38-39, Romans 8:9-11, John 14:21, Matthew 5:18, Matthew 5:21-48, Romans 8:1-4, Matthew 19:17, (See Table IV), Matthew 6:1, Matthew 5:6, Hebrews 6:1-3, Matthew 22:40, Romans 8:3, Matthew 19:18-19, Matthew 19:26, Matthew 19:29-30, Romans 8:4-5, John 3:8, I Peter 1:15-16, Leviticus 20:7, I John 2:16-17, Luke 9:23, Mark 8:34-35, Matthew 11:28-30

Lesson 8

Psalm 85:8, Galatians 6:2, Romans 10:17, John 14:21, Jer. 45:5, Matthew 11:30, I John 2:17

Lesson 9

Romans 12:9-21, Romans 10:17, Matthew 7:7, John 10:10, Philippians 4:6-7, Hebrews 6:19, Matthew 6:14-15, Ephesians 6:10-18, Romans 12:12, Matthew 6:1-6 & 16-21

Study Conclusion

Matthew 19:29-30, Matthew 5:43-48, Philippians 1:6, Matthew 25:31

Bibliograpy

"The Certainty of God's Promises" by Pastor Andrew Paton, A Sermon on Hebrews 6:13-20, (Part A: Hebrews 6:13-15), delivered August 12, 2012.

The Holiest of All by Andrew Murray, Copyright © 1996, 2004, Whitaker House, New Kensington, PA.

The New Testament in Modern English by J.B. Phillips, the final Revised Edition, Copyright © 1972 (The paraphrasing removed, this is a direct translation of the ancient Greek New Testament accomplished over a period of more than 20 years using the "latest and best" Greek texts available.); The Macmillan Company Publishers.

The New American Standard Bible (NASB), The Open Bible Edition, Copyright © 1960, 1962, 1963, 1968, 1971, 1972, 1975, 1977 The Lockman Foundation, Copyright © 1978, 1979 Thomas Nelson Publishers.

Holy Bible, King James Version (KJ), The World Publishing Company, Cleveland, OH.

Holy Bible, New International Version (NIV), Copyright © 1973, 1978, 1984 The International Bible Society, Zondervan Publishing House.

The Cost of Discipleship by Dietrich Bonhoeffer, First Touchstone Edition 1995, Copyright © 1949, 1959, 2001 by Simon and Schuster and SCM Press Ltd., Translated from the German *Nachfolge* first published in 1937 by Chr. Kaiser Verlag München by R. H. Fuller, with some revision by Irmgard Booth.

Discipleship by Dietrich Bonhoeffer, First Fortress Press Paperback Edition 2003, *Dietrich Bonhoeffer Works, Volume 4:* Copyright © 2001 Augsburg Fortress, Translated from the German Edition, Edited by Martin Kuske and Ilse Tödt, English Edition Edited by Geffrey B. Kelly and John D. Godsey, Translated by Barbara Green and Reinhard Krauss, Editor's Afterword to the German Edition.

T. C. PINKERTON

Bonhoeffer – Pastor, Martyr, Prophet, Spy by Eric Metaxas, Copyright © 2010 Thomas Nelson Inc., Nashville, TN.

Dietrich Bonhoeffer - Letters and Papers from Prison, The Enlarged Edition, Edited by Eberhard Bethge, First Touchstone Edition 1997, Published by Simon & Schuster, Copyright © 1953, 1967, 1971 by SCM Press Ltd.

REFERENCES

[1] *The New Testament in Modern English* by J. B. Phillips, Revised Edition, © 1972 The Macmillan Company, page 415.

[2] J. B. Phillips, ibid. page 461.

[3] J. B. Phillips, op. cit. page 459.

[4] J. B. Phillips, op. cit. page 461.

[5] The Amplified Bible, Updated Edition, © 1987 The Lockman Foundation, Zondervan Publishing House.

[6] Worldwide English New Testament, © 1996 SOON Educational Publishers.

[7] The idea of the "unpardonable" sin starting as a habit and leading to a lifestyle was suggested by Pastor Andrew Paton.

[8] A comment interjected by Pastor Andrew Paton.

[9] Taken from *The Holiest of All* by Andrew Murray. Copyright © 1996, 2004 Whitaker House. Used by permission. www.whitakerhouse.com Chapter 46 "Of Diligence and Perseverance" on Hebrews 6:9-12.

[10] Andrew Murray, ibid. page 225

[11] J. B. Phillips, op. cit. page 462.

[12] Revised Version of the King James New Testament of the Holy Bible, Oxford University Press (1881), Oxford, UK, passage from reference 9 on page 223.

[13] Andrew Murray, op. cit. page 224.

[14] Andrew Murray, op. cit. page 225.

[15] Andrew Murray, ibid.

[16] Andrew Murray, op. cit. page 223.

[17] *Worship in Song*, Nazarene Hymnal, © 1972 Lillenas Publishing Co., song 432.

[18] Revised Version of the King James, op. cit., passage from reference 9 on page 227.

[19] "The Certainty of God's Promises" by Pastor Andrew Paton, a sermon on Hebrews 6:13-20, (Part A: Heb 6:13-15), delivered August 12, 2012.

[20] Pastor Andrew Paton, ibid.

[21] Andrew Murray, op. cit. page 227.

[22] Andrew Murray, op. cit. page 228.

[23] Andrew Murray, op. cit. page 229.

[24] Andrew Murray, ibid.

[25] Andrew Murray, ibid.

[26] J. B. Phillips, op. cit. page 405.

[27] J. B. Phillips, op. cit. page 362.

[28] J. B. Phillips, op. cit. page 361.

29   J. B. Phillips, op. cit. page 363.

30   *Worship in Song*, Nazarene Hymnal, op. cit. song 303.

31   Andrew Murray, op. cit. page 236.

32   J. B. Phillips, op. cit. page 462.

33   Andrew Murray, op. cit. page 231.

34   Andrew Murray, op. cit. page 232.

35   Andrew Murray, ibid.

36   J. B. Phillips, op. cit. page 470.

37   Andrew Murray, op. cit. page 233.

38   J. B. Phillips, op. cit. page 470.

39   J. B. Phillips, op. cit., Philippians 3:12, page 415.

40   J. B. Phillips, op. cit., Philippians 3:13-14, page 415.

41   Andrew Murray, op. cit. page 235.

42   Andrew Murray, op. cit. page 236.

43   Andrew Murray, ibid.

44   Webster's II New Riverside University Dictionary, ©1984 Houghton Mifflin Co. p.1316.

45   Andrew Murray, op. cit. page 237.

46   Andrew Murray, ibid.

47   Andrew Murray, ibid.

48   *Worship in Song*, Nazarene Hymnal, op. cit., song 36.

49   J. B. Phillips, op. cit. page 495.

50   J. B. Phillips, op. cit. page 485.

51   J. B. Phillips, op. cit. page 439.

52   J. B. Phillips, op. cit. page 445.

53   J. B. Phillips, op. cit. page 409.

54   J. B. Phillips, op. cit. page 383.

55   J. B. Phillips, op. cit. page 444.

56   J. B. Phillips, op. cit. page 10.

57   J. B. Phillips, op. cit. page 11.

58   J. B. Phillips, ibid.

59   J. B. Phillips, op. cit. page 363.

60   J. B. Phillips, op. cit. page 362.

61   J. B. Phillips, op. cit. page 407.

62   J. B. Phillips, op. cit. page 461.

63   J. B. Phillips, op. cit. page 323.

64   J. B. Phillips, op. cit. page 439.

65   Scripture references: Matt. 22:37; Mark 12:30; Luke 10:27; Deut. 6:5, 10:12, Deut. 11:13, & 13:3.

66   Scripture references: Matt. 19:19, 22:39; Mark 12:5; Luke 10:27; Rom. 13:9, Gal. 5:14, James 2:8

67   Scripture reference: John 13:34-35

68   http://en.wikipedia.org/wiki/613_commandments

69   J. B. Phillips, op. cit. page 323.

70   In a letter from Dietrich Bonhoeffer to Eberhard Bethge, 21 July 1944; reprinted from page 369 with permission of Scribner Publishing Group, a division of Simon & Schuster, Inc., from *Dietrich Bonhoeffer Letters and Papers from Prison, Revised, The Enlarged Edition,*

Touchstone 1997, edited by Eberhard Bethge, translated from the German by R.H. Fuller, Frank Clark, et al. Copyright © 1953, 1967, 1971 by SCM Press Ltd. All rights reserved.

71   In a letter by Dietrich Bonhoeffer from Finkenwalde dated January 27, translated by Martin Kuske and Ilse Tödt as part of a biography in the Editors' Afterward to the German Edition of *Discipleship* by Dietrich Bonhoeffer 1937 and found in the First Fortress Press Paperback Edition 2003, *Dietrich Bonhoeffer Works*, Vol. 4: page 291, Copyright © 2001 Augsburg Fortress Press. This Afterward to the German Edition is not found in the English translation of *The Cost of Discipleship* by Dietrich Bonhoeffer, First Touchstone Edition 1995 published by Simon & Schuster, Inc., Copyright © 1959 by SCM Press Ltd.

72   *Dietrich Bonhoeffer Works*, Vol. 10, "Barcelona, Berlin, New York: 1928-1931", Edited by Clifford J. Green, Translated by Douglas W. Stott, Fortress Press, New York, 2008, page 201.

73   *Dietrich Bonhoeffer Works*, Vol. 13, "London: 1933-1935", Edited by Keith Clements, Translated by Isabel Best, Fortress Press, New York, 2007, page 126.

74   "Christians against Nazis: the German Confessing Church" by Leonore Siegele-Wenschkewitz, January 1986, an article in Christianity Today http://www.christianitytoday.com/ch/1986/issue9/9100.html

75   These excerpts are reprinted with permission of Scribner Publishing Group, a division of Simon & Schuster, Inc., from *The Cost of Discipleship* by Dietrich Bonhoeffer, First Touchstone Edition 1995, translated from the German *Nachfolge* by R.H. Fuller with revisions by Irmgard Booth, first published in 1937 by Chr. Kaiser Verlag München. Copyright © 1959 by SCM Press Ltd.

76   These excerpts are extracted from pages 63, 64, and 73 of *The Cost of Discipleship* by Dietrich Bonhoeffer, op. cit.

77   This excerpt is taken from pages 66-67 of *The Cost of Discipleship* by Dietrich Bonhoeffer, op. cit.

78   These two excerpts can be found on pages 4 and 5 of *Dietrich Bonhoeffer Letters and Papers from Prison*, edited by Eberhard Bethge, Touchstone 1997, op. cit.

79   *Bonhoeffer – Pastor, Martyr, Prophet, Spy* by Eric Metaxas, Copyright © 2010 Thomas Nelson, page 446.

80   This letter can be found on pages 369-370 of *Dietrich Bonhoeffer Letters and Papers from Prison,* edited by Eberhard Bethge, Touchstone 1997, op. cit.

81   *Love Letters from Cell 92: The Correspondence Between Dietrich Bonhoeffer and Maria Von Wedemeyer 1943-45*, Translated by John Brownjohn, Abringdon Press, New York, 1995, page 268.

82   *I Knew Dietrich Bonhoeffer*, Edited by Wolf-Deiter Zimmermann and Ronald G. Smith, Harper and Row, New York, 1966, page 227.

83   *Dietrich Bonhoeffer: A Biography* by Eberhard Bethge, Minneapolis: Fortress Press, 1967, page 927.

84   *Dr. Franz Hildebrandt: Mr. Valiant for Truth*, by Amos Cresswell and Maxwell Tow, Smyth and Helwys, Grand Rapids, 2000, page 226.

85   *Worship in Song*, Nazarene Hymnal, op. cit. song 33.

86   J. B. Phillips, op. cit. page 332-333.

87   J. B. Phillips, op. cit. page 10.

88   This quote is on pages 279-280 of *Discipleship* by Dietrich Bonhoeffer, op. cit.

Printed in the United States
By Bookmasters